Political Religion

POLITICAL RELIGION

A Liberal Answers the Question, "Should Politics and Religion Mix?"

Charles R. Stith

Abingdon Press
Nashville

POLITICAL RELIGION
A LIBERAL ANSWERS THE QUESTION,
"SHOULD POLITICS AND RELIGION MIX?"

Copyright © 1995 by Abingdon Press

This book is printed on recycled, acid-free paper.

Library of Congress Cataloging-in-Publication Data
Stith, Charles R.
    Political religion : a liberal answers the question, "Should politics and religion mix?" / Charles R. Stith.
        p.   cm.
    Includes bibliographical references.
    ISBN 0-687-00437-3 (alk. paper)
    1. Christianity and politics.   2. Liberalism (Religion)—United States.   3. Liberalism (Religion)—Protestant churches.
    4. Liberalism—United States.   5. United States—Church history—20th century.   6. United States—Politics and government—1993–   I. Title.
BR516.S83   1995
261.7'0973—dc20   95-33306
                                                           CIP

Scripture quotations, unless otherwise indicated are from the New Revised Standard Version Bible, copyright © 1989 by the Division of Christian Education of the National Council of the Churches of Christ in the United States of America.

Scripture quotations noted KJV are from the King James Version of the Bible.

Excerpts from *Prophetic Fragments* by Cornel West are used by permission of William B. Eerdmans Publishing Company.

Excerpts from *Before the Mayflower: A History of the Negro in America 1619–1964,* by Lerone Bennett, Jr., © 1962 Johnson Publishing Company, Inc.

95 96 97 98 99 00 01 02 03 04 — 10 9 8 7 6 5 4 3 2 1

MANUFACTURED IN THE UNITED STATES OF AMERICA

"To all the saints who from their labors rest":

Pearl Stith
Percy W. Prothrow Jr.
Mary Louise Thompson
Lady Percy Franklin
James Edward Butler
Major J. Jones

CONTENTS

Political Religion

ACKNOWLEDGMENTS

W hile I take full responsibility for the ideas and arguments put forth in this book, particularly the shortcomings or imperfections in style and substance, there are a number of people I must thank because their help was invaluable to its completion.

This project might well have not been pursued to publication without the encouragement of my friend of more than twenty years, the Reverend Joseph Washington. He read parts of the manuscript in its original form, and was persistent in his encouragement that I pursue publication of this book.

The editorial suggestions of my colleague and friend Leslie Belay were invaluable to the final form of this book. Her time and attention to detail honed the text into its present form.

Finally, I thank my family. The encouragement, support, and feedback from my wife, Deborah, was indispensable. The excitement over what I was trying to accomplish in this book by my children Percy, Mimi, and Trey; my mother, Dorothy, and my sister Becky; and my mother-in-law, Mildred, helped immensely. There were times when the frustration of this labor might have resulted in my laying this project aside had they not kept cheering me on.

POLITICAL RELIGION

I n the history of Western civilization the debate about the proper relationship of politics to religion is old. That debate has been particularly hot in this country over the last few years. *Political Religion* is a response to that debate.

I come to this debate as the former pastor of Union Church, one of the nation's oldest African American congregations. It is a United Methodist congregation tracing its first meetings to 1796. Historically, it served as a stop on the Underground Railroad. In modern times it has financed construction of low-income housing and sponsored high-intensity protests over United States involvement in South Africa.

During my tenure, Union's pulpit served as a forum for presidential candidates John Anderson, Gary Hart, Jesse Jackson, and Michael Dukakis, as well as political figures such as former First Lady Rosalynn Carter, former Democratic majority whip William Gray, UN Ambassador Andrew Young, Senator Ted Kennedy, Kansas City Mayor Emmanuel Cleaver, and prophetic leaders Coretta Scott King and Archbishop Desmond Tutu.

In 1985 I founded the Organization for a New Equality and continue to serve as its national president. The Organization for a New Equality is one of the nation's newest organizations dedicated to the cause of economic justice. Through its National Community Reinvestment Network it has leveraged over $60 billion in commitments for community reinvestment.

Political Religion reflects the sum of my experiences of political involvement—from protest to political action, from voter registration to policy formulation. This book reflects the initiatives taken and insights gained over the years as a result of discussions with political candidates and political leaders. This book reflects what I've seen and learned from having visited countries such as South Africa, Zimbabwe, Nicaragua, Honduras, and Japan to evaluate the effects of this country's foreign policies.

This book is a statement about how the church ought to be the purveyor of the "politics of inclusion, justice, and equality." This statement needs to be made because over the past several years we have witnessed a frightening increase of racial tension and violence in our communities, on college campuses, and in the world community.

The 1890s were referred to as the "Terrible Nineties." It was an era noteworthy for its introduction of apartheid American-style; we called that period the "Jim Crow Era." Racial violence and oppression reached epidemic proportions. The 1990s have the same potential. In the 1890s, a Black man could be lynched for being accused of looking *at* a White woman. On the threshold of the 1990s, in Bensonhurst, New York, a young Black man was shot dead for being suspected of looking *for* a White woman.

Even more recently, former Ku Klux Klan Grand Wizard David Duke used the shroud of born-again Christianity to cloak his racist campaign for governor of the state of Louisiana. In an interview in the *New York Times* he characterized affirmative action and welfare as evidence that "Christian values are under attack." Though he lost the election, he received 55 percent of the White vote in an election in which over 80 percent of the electorate went to the polls.

It is clear that as a nation we have not crossed the racial divide that separates us, and it is a threat to our nation. We must forge a new consensus around the need for a national commitment to a just and equitable life together. This vision of a nation that is harmonious, just, and equitable must be the standard by which to judge our political, economic, and social behavior. *Political Religion* is an examination of how the problems of racism, discrimination, and injustice encroach on our common life, and it is an identification of theological underpinnings for racial harmony, justice, and equality.

I first started thinking about this subject as a possible book in 1976. It was the year presidential candidate Jimmy Carter listed his status as a born-again Christian as one of his political credentials. In 1980, President Carter and a select number of liberal members of Congress on the religious right's hit list were defeated. A striking example of the conflict and controversy regarding politics and religion was the presidential candidacies of the Reverends Jesse Jackson and Pat Robertson in 1988. With right-wing religious fundamentalists, the Catholic Church, the liberal Protestant community, and the Black Church seemingly still committed to involvement in the political process, the controversy over the church's political involvement will continue to be fired to fever pitch.

Political Religion is written as an emphatic "Yes!" to the question, "Should politics and religion mix?" It is a statement, as Robert McAfee Brown notes in his recent book

Spirituality and Liberation, that "one can believe that religion and politics do mix without being persuaded that every 'mix' is a good one."[1]

Political Religion is a call for a commitment to justice, harmony, and opportunity on a wide range of issues critical to our times. It is written for religious-minded people who seek to understand, or are inclined to give serious thought to what it means to be authentically religious and politically active. It is written for people for whom the issue of politics and religion is of interest, for whatever reason.

Political Religion is, in part, a personal story of my political involvements and a response to the interest in religion and politics created by recent political campaigns. In the final analysis, I hope the value of this book is its helpful response to people who have deeply felt moral concerns that must be worked out in a political context.

POLITICS
AND
RELIGION

Generally speaking, Christian people agree that they ought to be active in the world. A funny story punctuates this point.

A church member who had not attended for a while was quite exuberant in worship upon his return. One Sunday he was especially moved. He started shouting during the procession. When the choir sang its first selection, "Amazing Grace," he was rocking and shouting "Yes, Lord, we know it's amazing" before they were a third of the way through the song. When the minister started preaching, he wasn't two minutes past the prayer before the member rose to his feet saying, "Tell the truth, brother, preach!" Then, after the minister had finished preaching, it was time to take up the offering. The preacher started by saying, "This church is really all we have," and the member responded, "It's all we have; thank you, Jesus." Then the minister said, "It needs to be stronger," and the member responded, "Yes, Lord, it needs to be stronger." And then the minister, having established a rhythm, said, "If it's going to be strong, you have got to give, give, give!" And he paused, expecting, at the least, an affirmation from the member who had been shouting all along. But, instead, the member was sitting passively on the pew singing, "Jesus paid it all!" This story highlights the absurdity of thinking there is no accountability in discipleship.

While Jesus has indeed paid a price for our salvation, discipleship has a cost as well. By definition, the church is about doing. Ernst Troeltsch underscores this in *The Social Teaching of the Christian Churches* by stating that "Christianity is first and foremost a matter of practice."[1] The church is called to be actively engaged in the world. But the ever-present question is, "What ought to be the thrust of the church's action?"

Liberation theologies have raised the standards for theological legitimacy and missional credibility. From the vantage point of liberation theology, "religion is understood as the means of the search for both individual and communal fulfillment beyond the alienation of our present existence. God's loyalties and humanity's lamentations are not for order, peace, and universality, but for justice, equity, and harmony. Because these ethical requirements are affirmed within the body politic, the church is clearly called to be involved politically. Politics is the arena in which "Christian truth becomes praxis."[2]

Simply asserting that the church should be involved politically is nothing new. Troeltsch describes the historical correspondence between the body politic and the body religious in the Western world. As examples, he cites the Reformed political doctrine of the Huguenots; the Congregationalists' participation of the free individual in the power of the state on the basis of religious freedom of conscience; and the French Declaration of the Rights of Man, and its connection with the American Constitution based on Congregational principles.[3]

Even church critics like the late Michael Harrington acknowledge the interface between church and state. In one of his later and more provocative works, *The Politics of God's Funeral: The Spiritual Crisis of Modern Civilization*, Harrington rightly discerns that while the God of the Judeo-Christian West has "omniscience, omnipotence, and all the rest," his existence has been political as well. This God is and has been:

- the legitimization of established power and sometimes of revolt against it;
- the transcendent symbol of the common consciousness of an existing community; . . .
- the organizing principle of a system of the authoritative allocation of social roles (the God of Western feudalism) or the motivating and ethical principle of a system of individual mobility (the God of Western capitalism);
- the guarantor of personal, ethnic and national identity.[4]

In short, a God-consciousness permeates every aspect of our nation's cultural, political, and economic life.

Even clearer than Harrington's typologies is the correspondence between the customs and creeds, symbols and rituals of the nation, and the confession, credos, and character of the religious community. Certainly, the periodic worship services at the White House, and the rituals of congressional, gubernatorial, and mayoral prayer breakfasts are affirmations of the interests shared by the religious and political communities. A significant mark of the interface between religiosity and national ritual is the use of the Bible in oath-taking for every office from president to justice of the peace. The reference to our being "one nation under God" as recited in the Pledge of Allegiance, as well as the notation on our money notes that it is "in God we trust," betrays a symbiotic understanding of church and state.

An even more poignant example of the interface between church and state, or religion and politics, is reflected in the Black church. Historically, the Black church has been the spawning ground for political movements and leadership. During the tragic days of slavery in this country, all sorts of political action—abolitionism, the Underground Railroad, insurrection—found support and succor in the Black church. With the abolition of slavery, schools and colleges were founded and furthered by the church. At the end of Reconstruction, the political philosophies of Black Nationalism and Pan-Africanism matured within the matrix of the Black church. In the modern era, it has again been the church advocating everything from civil rights to voter registration to the legitimacy of Jimmy Carter's presidential candidacy.

The list of political leaders born and bred in the Black church is as impressive as it is significant. Frederick Douglass, an abolitionist and the first Black of ambassadorial rank in the United States, was an ordained minister. The insurrectionist Nat Turner was called to his mission to overthrow slavery, a mission ordained by God. Hiram Revels, who served in the United States Senate during the era of Reconstruction, was a clergyman. Bishop Henry McNeil Turner, of the AME Church, was one of the forerunners of Pan-Africanist thought. All of today's civil rights legislation came about as a result of a movement led by a Black Baptist minister named Martin Luther King Jr.

20

Some of the most adamant advocates for the poor in the political arena have been Black clergymen: Adam Clayton Powell, Walter Fauntroy, Floyd Flake, John Lewis, Andrew Young, Emmanuel Cleaver, and Bill Gray, to name a few. From the pulpit, contemporary prophets have been legion: Kirbyjon Caldwell, Charles Adams, Leontine Kelly, Cecil Williams, Barbara Harris, Tony Stanley, Edgar Boyd, Jesse Boyd, Gary Simpson, H. Beecher Hicks, Nelson Thompson, Johnny Youngblood, John Bryant, Mickarl Thomas, Howard Creecy Sr., and Howard Creecy Jr., Charles Coverdale, Walter Kimbrough, Joe Roberts, Joe Lowery, and others.

• • •

In my own life, the mixing of politics and religion has seemed natural. I grew up in the Black church. In the Black church the songs, Bible stories, and preaching addressed the political situation of Black people and poor people. The message of those African American spirituals I heard on Sunday morning was that my political status as a second-class citizen was inconsistent with my ontological or spiritual status as an equal to anyone in the sight of God.

Spirituals like "Oh, Freedom" captured that sentiment for me. The point of the song was that my lack of political standing should be challenged. The Exodus story helped me to understand the Bible and my standing as a Black person in America. Tying the sentiment of spirituals and the interpretation of Exodus together was the preacher who "talked the talk and walked the walk," that is, he challenged and led us in the ways of hope and freedom.

Aside from being nurtured on a steady diet of African American spirituals with implicitly political themes, Old Testament stories that emphasized God's inclination to take the "rejected stone" as the "cornerstone" for a new kingdom, and a preacher who kept our minds on freedom, I came of age in an era dominated by the vision of a preacher named Martin Luther King Jr. It was an era in which change in the nation's political life was evidence of the power of the church. Being born on the cusp of profound change, and now standing on the cutting edge of even more change, I have always seen the church involved in politics. All that I have known is the church influencing political values and claiming political victories. From my vantage point, being religious means being political; that one's politics reflects one's religion is not an option, but an obligation.

The present controversy over mixing politics and religion is a conflict about whether religion should influence politics at all; and, if so, on what terms. In this chapter, I expand on my perspective and present a conceptual framework for understanding the proper relationship between religion and politics. In so doing, I address three significant questions: (1) What is at the heart of the present controversy over mixing politics and religion? (2) How do we resolve the present controversy? and (3) What is the religious and political agenda for our time?

The Present Controversy

The public, and politically sensitive, argument in which Americans are engaged about the role of religion in political life essentially reflects a struggle for power. The argument is not simply about whether religion ought to influence politics, though many couch the present controversy in those terms. The present controversy over religion and politics is really a fight about *whose* religion and *whose*

22

politics. It is a battle between the political left and the political right, liberals and conservatives, new ideologies and old ideologies, new orthodoxies and old orthodoxies, progressive forces and oppressive forces.

The source of the present controversy is that the political right, which includes Christian Fundamentalists, has launched a rearguard assault against the liberal political establishment to regain the political hegemony that was once theirs. Over the past thirty years, despite the fact that we have had four moderate-to-conservative Republican presidents, liberal values have defined the context of political debate from the right to privacy to equal opportunity.

The political preeminence of the left over the last thirty years is the legacy of a church-inspired Civil Rights Movement. Therefore, Christian Fundamentalists are right to cry foul when those to the left of center protest their involvement in politics on the grounds that politics and religion don't mix. On the other hand, the Fundamentalists do overstate their case when they argue that until their recent foray into politics our political life was without moral content. That has never been the case.

This was a morals/values statement

Those on the Christian right like to contend that for years they were like the "country Christian" the late Representative Brooks Hays joked about, who when confronted by a pollster about his preference for an upcoming election said: "I'm a Christian and I have never voted in my life and I never intend to. It might just encourage them." The reality is that from the Hayes-Tilden Compromise of 1876, which marked the end of Reconstruction, until the Montgomery Movement of 1955, "good Christian White folk" held a monopoly on political power in the South and patterned the political ethos for the nation on matters of race and justice. Feeling justified by "Christian

23

duty," they changed laws and Blacks were systematically oppressed. On matters of race, conservatism was the metronome to which the nation marched.

The present controversy over mixing religion and politics is not about the Christian right's political efforts to interject morals into our political life. The problem for those of us to the left of center is that their power play is predicated on outdated precepts. The Christian right uses some code words reminiscent of the Jim Crow Era. Their political equation has two factors, Us (Christian Patriots) versus Them (humanists, homosexuals, people of color, criminals, and liberals), and this equation is defined by conflict rather than reconciliation. Their convictions—the impetus for Constitutional amendments on abortion, school prayer, and taxes—are the problem.

To state the present controversy differently, the issue of mixing religion and politics in America is whether there are religious values that enable the perfection of American democracy instead of simply propagating a particular sect's view of Christian piety. I say yes; there is a way to mix religion and politics such that we preclude a sectarian bias in the way we live our political lives. The proper mix of politics and religion that results from the "perfection" of democracy requires us to give priority to justice, harmony, and opportunity.

Raising these values to prominence ought to be the contemporary political agenda of the church. The agenda that I am proposing has its roots in our theological and philosophical tradition. I suggest that this historic philosophical and theological link between Western Christianity and American democracy is the key to resolving the present controversy.

24

Resolving the Present Controversy

Let me define what I mean by church and religion (terms that I use interchangeably). There are two ways to define church and religion. One is the common understanding of church and religion as an institution of faith or a force in people's lives. Its raison d'être is God. It is the dogma and doctrine around which believers organize their lives and that makes the church as an organization live. As an individual I am the church, as a believer and as an African American ordained United Methodist minister. The church is also the institution I pastor, the denomination to which I belong, and the other sects and denominations that make up the "body of Christ." Within the context of this book, when I talk about the church and religion, I mean this and something more.

The second way to define church and religion is political. This definition focuses on the interface between faith and the broader social and cultural context in which the Christian community lives.

According to this definition, the church and religion embodies the vision and the values it brings to bear as a participant in the political process. The *vision* and *values* that are projected and defended are certainly rooted in the Christian tradition, but not limited to this religious tradition or any particular philosophical tradition. Indeed, the most appropriate religious values for informing our political behavior are those values that are common to the philosophical and constitutional tradition of this country.

The second definition of the church and religion is the rationale for the case I make in this book. This definition is the sense of itself that the church must master to be

25

effective and fair in an ethnically pluralistic and religiously diverse democracy such as ours.

Not only is there a contemporary necessity for understanding the church in this way; there is also a historical basis for advocating such an understanding. When surveying the landscape of Christian belief, there are obvious sectarian differences and emphases, but there is also a thread that connects Western Christianity to American democracy. That thread is a central ideal that undergirds both. Ernst Troeltsch, in a paper entitled "Political Ethics and Christianity," details the compatibility between democracy and Christianity:

> The democratic principle implies a world view, a metaphysics, and a religion. . . . A certain ethic is implied here, namely the ethic of justice and love toward all. . . . This ethic sees [everyone] as springing from a single root and aspiring to a single goal to see the idea of humanity actualized in every individual.[5]

Troeltsch rightly discerns that there is a close connection between democratic ideals and Christianity springing from a common ethical concern. He notes:

> During its formative period, modern democracy received the strongest impulses from Puritan circles and the Reformed ideal of popular sovereignty. Even . . . Catholicism justifies its extensive recognition of democracy by the Christian belief in the person. Protestant groups regard their alliance with democracy as a moral obligation for the sake of the gospel, and social democracy claims for its own the true historical Jesus. Indeed, the Christian feeling that the poor and humble must be supported in their aspirations is generally the ally of contemporary democracy.[6]

26

In a nutshell, Troeltsch is saying that there is a fundamental principle common to democracy and Christianity.
The basic premise underlying each is that all individuals
have equal intrinsic worth. Because a basic assumption of
Christianity and democracy is that we are equals, what we
give and get in our personal and political relationships
must reflect a sense of justice. Justice is the authentic
measure for the quality of relationships. As equals there
must be a balance between our respective needs and
wants. In other words, there is no prima facie preference
(based on color, class, or gender) for one individual will
over another; the only issue that ought to matter in nego-
tiating issues and concerns is, What is just? This premise
is affirmed again and again in America's documentary
history—from the Declaration of Independence to the
Voting Rights Act of 1965 to the Civil Rights Act of 1991—
and has been voiced from America's pulpits and pews again
and again.

This affinity between democracy and Christianity is
doubly significant for the church's involvement in politics.
The principle of equal worth shared by Christianity and
democracy defines the objective of political participation
and policy formulation: public policies must be just, and
political action must be directed to addressing the justice
issue and electing politicians committed to a justice
agenda.

In the present debate on the role of religion in politics,
the intrinsic equal worth of persons must be protected. In
the words of Martin Luther King Jr., "Men will be judged
not by the color of their skin, but by the content of their
character."

Understanding that there is a common ideal that undergirds democracy and Christianity and acting on that under-

27

standing enables us to stand with a foot in both traditions. From that vantage point, the view offers profound implications for how the political and religious agenda for our time is understood. The focus of that agenda, simply put, is to ensure that justice is done. We will explore the implications of this agenda later in the chapter.

While the principle of equal worth is the religious and political ideal, we must remember that all too often in the real world "those that have, get; and those that have not, get not." This political reality requires the church to serve as the corrective—to insist that the "rejected stone" become the "cornerstone" of our political concern and public policy agenda.

Jürgen Moltmann, in *On Human Dignity*, contends that the church has a messianic agenda and that messianic activity must encompass the following:

1. The struggle for economic justice against the exploitation of some people by other people.
2. The struggle for human rights and freedom against the political oppression of some people by other people.
3. The struggle for human solidarity against the cultural, the racist, and the sexist alienation of people from people.
4. The struggle for ecological peace with nature against the industrial destruction of nature by human beings.
5. The struggle for assurance against apathy in personal life.

These five dimensions hang so close together that there can be no economic justice without political freedom, no improvement of socioeconomic conditions without over-coming cultural alienation and without personal conversion from apathy to hope. Whoever does not understand salvation in the most comprehensive literal sense and does not strive for a network of saving anticipations over the various fields of devastation does not understand salvation holistically.[7]

In the context of American politics, those for whom the church must engage in the sort of messianic activity Molt-mann describes is clear. Those holding the short end of the stick are easily identified along color, class, gender, and generation lines. The church, as it has historically done, must use the moral and institutional power at its disposal on behalf of those who are defined by the powerful as powerless. This agenda has its roots in church tradition, the Bible, and the church's prophetic task as reflected in its sense of revelation and faith.

Church Tradition: Old Text or New?

Beyond understanding our political situation, reference points within the church's tradition are critical to legitimiz-ing the church's political agenda. The church's political agenda must be rooted in Christian tradition if it is going to have the support of parishioners and have the power to be effective. Where in the ecclesiastical past do we look for signposts for present and future political action? Who in the tradition do we trust to signal direction in our situation?

José Miguez Bonino, in his book *Toward a Christian Political Ethic*, offers a point of departure. Analyzing the political theology of Augustine, Bonino critiques patriar-chal theology in Western culture. He contends:

29

Augustine saw history as the place where God's city and the human city intersect, struggle and move toward their particular appointed goals. Justice and love are two foundations of the eternal city that impinge on the earthly one. . . . Justice (the objective basis) and love (the motivating force) together offer a hermeneutical key that enables us to discern God's active presence in history and to determine our Christian praxis accordingly.[8]

So far so good, as Bonino notes. But as Augustine begins to confront the concrete problems of oppression, injustice, and poverty, this hermeneutical key loses much of its meaning. Bonino observes that Augustine dictates the redress of such wrongs "without endangering the order and peace." Augustine's position here is quite clear: peace implies order. Bonino goes on to critique Augustine's implicit hermeneutical bias, which subsumes all ethical interpretations to the hierarchy of order—an order that Augustine claims reflects the natural order of the universe. As Bonino notes, Augustine's concept of order draws upon the classical Greco-Roman tradition, which views human society as a natural organism (in Plato or Aristotle "the celestial order"). In this system the hierarchy of basic "organs," or parts, is naturally determined and regulated—government and subjects, citizens and slaves, men and women. In the classical view, any disruption of these hierarchical relations is a crime against nature, and in Christian theology, a rebellion against creation. Thus, in the Augustinian framework, peace is understood as order and is the ultimate key to determining political action. Bonino summarizes his point this way: "Theologically, justice and love are supreme, but historically both are subordinate to order."[9]

The Augustinian principle of hierarchy for political participation still permeates Western theology and philosophy. I contend that a proper political hermeneutic requires a reversal of that scheme. Order must be subordinate to justice! Jesus said, "I have not come to bring peace, but a sword" (Matt. 10:34). David Tracy, contemporary Catholic theologian, notes that "the memory of Jesus disconcerts all present reality, including that of the Church, because He essentially afflicts the comfortable and comforts the afflicted."[10]

If classical theology offers an approach that equivocates on issues of justice, then where do we look for leadership? I suggest the Black church. The Black church today is the word of God, the text, interpreted through action—the quintessential hermeneutical task. Tracy recognizes this as the Black church's historical response to its political situation: "We know from the spirituals and blues that the Black slaves in our own country had a correct reading for Exodus." This root has flowered in the institutional Black church.

Cornel West, in *Prophesy Deliverance*,[11] details the development of a justice agenda in the theology of the African American church. West delineates the evolution of three typologies of Black theology; theologies that evolved through three stages in deep connection with the life of the Black church. His analysis indicates that the Black church has set a historical precedent for church action. West's stages of Black theological development suggest a clear direction for the church's political vision and mission:

The first stage can be viewed roughly as *Black Theology of Liberation as a Critique of Slavery.* This stage, lasting approximately from the middle of the seventeenth century to 1863, consisted of Black prophetic Christian viewpoints and actions that were grounded in the Black slave experience and were critical of the institution of slavery. The prophetic Christian view was that the gospel stands unequivocally opposed to slavery.

The second stage can be viewed as *Black Theology of Liberation as a Critique of Institutional Racism*. This stage, which occupied more than a century (1864–1969), found Black prophetic Christians principally focusing attention on the racist institutional structures in the United States. This structural racism, which the Black church attacked, rendered the vast majority of Black people politically powerless (deprived of the right to vote or participate in governmental affairs), economically exploited (in dependent positions as sharecroppers or in unskilled jobs), and socially degraded (separate, segregated, and unequal in eating and recreational facilities, housing, education, transportation, and police protection).

With the publishing of Albert Cleage's *Black Messiah* (1968) and James Cone's *Black Theology and Black Power* (1969), a third stage commenced: *Black Theology of Liberation as a Critique of White American Theology*. This stage was an intellectually creative one—partly in response to the spontaneous rebellion of Black people in the streets, the more disciplined political praxis of Black Power groups, and the paralysis of most White North American theologians.

As West illustrates, the African American Christian tradition has consistently interpreted the word of God as a political theology, giving justice the priority it deserves. The Black church's precedent authenticates a justice agenda for the church and a historical standard for judging its present political agenda.

32

Biblical Tradition and the Church: Accommodation or Apocalypse?

The biblical tradition has critically shaped the church's reflection and action. By tradition and technique, churchfolk are a biblical people. It is critical that we understand ourselves in terms of what the Bible says we ought to be; and that we see our action as grounded in what the Bible says we ought to do. The church requires a biblical hermeneutic to substantiate its political agenda.

Historically, the Western Church has seized upon a political hermeneutic for interpreting the Bible that has been focused upon one of two poles. Either the emphasis has been on *accommodation* as identified with the thirteenth chapter of Romans; or the emphasis has been on *apocalypse* as identified with the thirteenth chapter of Revelation. The Romans chapter begins:

> Let every soul be subject unto the higher powers. For there is no power but of God: the powers that be are ordained of God. Whosoever therefore resisteth the power, resisteth the ordinance of God: and they that resist shall receive to themselves damnation. (KJV)

In stark contrast, Revelation 13:10 reads:

> He that leadeth into captivity shall go into captivity: he that killeth with the sword must be killed with the sword. Here is the patience and the faith of the saints. (KJV)

These passages stand out most clearly in dialogue and discourse on biblical politics. With no intention of engaging in a detailed exegetical exercise I simply introduce these passages as foci of biblical politics.

33

However, each of these positions is inadequate because each ignores the believer's interpretive act: the commitment and advocacy that emerges through faith. Rather than a political hermeneutic that focuses on accommodation or apocalypse, our concern should be what the Bible says about allegiance. On whose side do you stand and for what do you stand? In the political arena where there are winners and losers, the critical question to which the biblical witness must respond is, "Whose side are you on?" Asking the question this way moves us beyond accommodationist and apocalyptic politics.

The holy writ is a story for the distressed, disinherited, and the denied. Lest there be any confusion, this does not pertain only to the spiritual realm; it relates also to the political, material, and historical realms. The Black church has historically embraced this as its biblical hermeneutic. Noted Black churchman and AME Bishop John Hurst Adams explains this well in his definition of what the Black church has been:

> First of all, the place where the Black Church was born and had to live forced it not to succumb to the dual definitions of reality the Church so often talks about. . . . We never fell victim to forced demarcations in our existence on earth, because the God we serve is a God of the spirit as well as the material, the God of politics. He is the God of both Church and state. Secondly, the government which governs us has authorities and powers which impact so decisively upon our daily lives that we must address them if we are to keep faith with the mission and the purpose of the Church. . . . Without the constraining presence of a spiritual and moral force, government always becomes the instrument of bondage.[12]

34

Political activity has been integral to the Black church's raison d'être because we have understood the Bible as a pronouncement against injustice. Dr. Cain Felder, in his landmark study, *Troubling Biblical Waters*,[13] makes the point that in the earliest sermons preached by Black preachers and the earliest theological literature of the Black church (i.e., the African American spiritual), it is clear that the Bible is understood as a freedom document. We must read the Bible—from beginning to end—as a call for justice. The wandering Aramean Abraham is promised plenty, the Israelite nation seeks freedom from Egyptian bondage, the prophet calls for "justice [to] roll down like waters, and righteousness like an everflowing stream" (Amos 5:24) culminating in Jesus' unequivocal commitment to justice: "The Spirit of the Lord is upon me, because he has anointed me to bring good news to the poor. He has sent me to proclaim release to the captives and recovery of sight to the blind, to let the oppressed go free, to proclaim the year of the Lord's favor" (Luke 4:18-19).

The Bible calls us to stand in the midst of the "least of them," not simply as sacerdotal functionaries presiding over their misery, but as prophets enabling, empowering, and advocating a just and equitable order.

Revelation and the Justice Agenda

The capacity to see God present in one's situation, traditionally understood as revelation, is at the core of our political agenda. Revelation entails discerning the "touch of the Master's hand" at a particular historic moment. To understand how we are to discern God's involvement in our affairs and how that determines our political agenda, let me begin by defining my understanding of revelation.

35

As I define revelation, it has two dimensions. It is like viewing a picture painted by God. The scenery in the picture is the context, and the subjects (perhaps including ourselves) are the content.

In order to understand what I mean by revelation as *context*, Paul Tillich's description of *kairos* is helpful.[14] Tillich identifies kairos as the context for revelation. It is time in the qualitative sense; it is that breakthrough in time when it is possible to receive a manifestation of the kingdom of God. We talk about this context colloquially as the moment when "it seems that something is in the air"; we talk about it poetically as that "magic moment." Biblically, it is the time Jesus referred to when he said that his time was yet to come. To give it an explicitly political character, revelation takes place when one knows a moment to be pregnant with possibility, when we stand to be midwives to a more just order. It is that moment when God—recognized in our midst—empowers our actions.

This sort of understanding of the context for action is arrived at by possibilities being revealed and not researched. It is a matter of "those with eyes, let them see." I call this revelation because, on the one hand, kairos is about all the parts played by the individual players at a particular historic moment. On the other hand, kairos has nothing to do with the parts played by the individual players, because the possibilities revealed are far greater than the sum of the parts of the players. For example, when Martin Luther King Jr. took up Rosa Parks's cause in Montgomery in 1955, no one knew that it would result in the most significant affirmation of this nation's loftiest ideals and change the political landscape so dramatically. But the time was right! When Jesse Jackson announced his first run for the White House in 1983, few really appreciated the extent to which the disinherited and disenfranchised would come alive and hope again. Jackson's campaign inspired the masses and interrupted business as usual. It happened because the time was right.

Research and analysis are critical to political action; that is, we must search for the signs of the times. But, we must not forget we are able to accomplish much because of the *spirit* of the times. As critical as research and analysis are, Martin Luther King Jr. often said that many a moment was lost because we were gripped by the "paralysis of analysis." If we are not to miss the moment, we must see God present in it! For this we can look, but we see only because it is shown; we can analyze, but we know only because it is revealed. When we talk about "the moment" or the spirit of the times with the language of mystery, we are looking with an inner eye, hearing with an inner ear. This is revelation.

To understand how the church is to act, we rely upon revelation as a clarification of the context, the backdrop. But, if we are to get a full picture, we must also discern the details. This is revelation as *content* and is the act of interpretation, insofar as we are subjects in God's painting.

As an illustration, this notion can best be understood by referring to Matthew 25:31-46. F. W. Beare, in his commentary on Matthew, calls this passage the "apocalyptic vision."[15] The story details the basis for ultimate judgment by God at the end of time. It begins on the day of "glory" when all the nations are gathered at the feet of the Most High. Those who inherit the keys of the kingdom are those who fed the hungry, gave drink to the thirsty, and clothed the naked. Those who had not done so had not seen Christ in the hungry and harried. Revelation provided the content for the actions of the righteous, opening their eyes to see Christ in the crises of individual persons and peoples.

To know how to act politically, the church needs to get the picture—the backdrop, the broad strokes, and the details. We, the church, must see Christ dictating our agenda in the tears, torment, and tattered lives of those we encounter. This is revelation, and for the church it is basic political information. We cannot respond to every case of injustice we see on an individual basis; but we can respond politically and effect public policy that promotes human development rather than human deprivation.

The Political and Religious Agenda for Our Time

As I have suggested, the political and religious agenda for our time is justice. Because of class and cultural elements that define discrimination and oppression in America, the political movement that most closely approximates the church's political agenda is populism. I say *approximates* because as a political movement within the context of American political history populism has left something to be desired. Cornel West, in an article titled "The New Populism: A Black Socialist Christian Critique," accurately describes the limits of populism as practiced in American politics. He writes:

> A central paradox of American populism is that it invests great confidence in the goodwill of the American people. Yet, from a black perspective, it has been primarily when the federal courts and government has "imposed" its laws upon the American people that there has been some black progress. It is important to note that the two major public acts associated with black progress—the Emancipation

Proclamation (1863) and the *Brown v. Board of Education* case (1954)—were far removed from the collective will of the American people. In fact, Congress would not have passed either if consulted and both would have lost in a national referendum.

Another paradox of American populism is that its attractive theme of empowerment rarely is inclusive enough to take black interests seriously. This is so not solely because of the racist sentiments of populist activists but, more importantly, because these activists must pursue their many goals within the American political system which forces populists to prioritize their goals and demands. Given this political context of limited options, populists (even those with the least racist sensibilities!) tend to sacrifice the interests of minorities to that of the majority. The strange career of Tom Watson—from left populist to the Ku Klux Klan—is exemplary in this regard. And less dramatic examples dot the landscape of American history.[16]

As practiced in American politics, populism has had a blind spot concerning whose interests to protect. But its underlying sentiment gets us close to where we want to be in our effort to understand what the church's political agenda ought to be. The primary appeal of populism is its plebeian bias. Given the fundamental principle of equal worth to both Christianity and democracy, and the church's concomitant obligation to be an advocate for the "least of those" in our midst, a way of summarizing the church's political agenda would be to call it "Christian Populism."

The notion of Christian Populism seems to be the most precise political expression of the religious agenda for our time. To conceptualize the church's political agenda in this way moves us beyond one of the primary problems of American populism, that is, prioritizing the political agenda based on the interests of the majority over protecting the interests of minorities. The emphasis of Christian populism starts with the advocacy of the interests of minorities and women (as the least advantaged class).

This does not mean that the interests of the majority (or men) are ignored or subsumed; it simply means that Christian Populism takes seriously the most fundamental law of the universe: everything grows from the bottom up and not from the top down. In political terms, if justice is assured for the least of those, it is protected for everyone else. This is also the basis for our country's Bill of Rights.

To frame this point in a manner consistent with today's justice issues, the crisis in public education is not simply a matter of desegregation versus neighborhood schools as the way to quality education. The question is whether Black and Hispanic children will have equitable access to educational resources. In foreign policy (the present realignment in Eastern Europe notwithstanding), the issue is not whether autocratic communism or democratic capitalism will prevail. The question is whether the people will be able to determine the political and economic destiny of their own countries. The economic issue domestically, particularly during times of recession, is not whether recession is the necessary cure for inflation. The question is when will we move beyond a policy of "last hired, first fired"—a policy precluding participation in the economic mainstream by those historically shut out.

It is in understanding these realities that the agenda of the church becomes ever more clear: move the powerless to power, the oppressed to equality, and replace discrimination with justice. This agenda is the means to human selfhood and the fundamental principle of Christianity and democracy. This is the essential concern of Christian Populism!

POLITICS AND RELIGION

But for Christian Populism to have legitimacy within the church, being relevant within the present political situation and our political tradition is not enough. If Christian Populism is going to have legitimacy in the church it must be grounded in faith.

A final consideration for the church's political action is a conviction that emerges from one's faith. God is the final arbiter of history. A churchperson who enters the political fray with any other perspective is in trouble. Faith is the starting point because in politics you play to win; but the fact of the matter is that sometimes you lose. If one presumes that history rests solely on winning particular elections or political battles, then one can become more concerned with the outcome at the polls and similar political outcomes than with the outcome on principle.

In a political situation all we can do is the best we can do, and believe that God will do the rest. In this sense, the political arena becomes a context for redemption. To work in this way is an act of faith. This is all we can do.

We act out of faith because, while we seek clarity before we act, often the signs are obscured. While we strive for a full picture, we rarely see the whole. We live in an era in which we are bombarded with so much information that one can never know all the facts. No matter how well versed one may be in scripture, biblical misinterpretation in the heat of passion is a trap that snares even the most fit. As we survey church tradition for those who have personified a hope for the ages, we find there have been and will be false prophets. Also, we must confess that we are all guilty of romanticizing the past; from time to time, all of us have become makeup artists covering history's warts. Signposts from the past can always be misread, and we can wind up headed in the wrong direction. We might

41

look carefully to discern the brushstrokes of the Master in the picture of our moment, but none of us is expert enough to verify the entire message. God paints many pictures, but what we see is not always what is there. I identify all of these qualifications to our calling because in the final analysis our political action is "a leap of faith." Political action is faith-action because we are responding to God's call, and I believe that if we are true to the call we will be vindicated in time.

CHAPTER TWO

THE CIVIL RIGHTS MOVEMENT
A New Epoch in Church History

During the Civil Rights Movement, the church offered a contemporary religious paradigm for political action. The church's leadership, personified in Martin Luther King Jr., included a model of the principles that ought to inform the church's political involvement and a model for implementation of those principles as praxes. What the church did during that period was the precursor of what I am calling Christian populism.

This chapter examines the historical-political context in which the Movement took place, analyzes the Movement as church history, and explores the impact of the "new moral order" advanced during the Movement. Two primary questions will be addressed: "Was the Movement a precursor for new standards and a different political configuration?" and "Did it give rise to a redistribution of political power?"

The Movement in Political History

For a generation for whom the Civil Rights Movement is history, Martin Luther King Jr. is a historic figure, racism is taboo, and Blacks are guaranteed equal protection under the law. Appreciating the significance of the Movement requires viewing it in the context in which it occurred.

During the all too brief interlude of freedom after the Civil War—the Reconstruction period—life looked better for Blacks. There was full citizenship with the passage of the Thirteenth, Fourteenth, and Fifteenth Amendments to the Constitution, along with the passage of the Civil Rights Act of 1875. The educational empowerment of the former slaves was advanced by the founding of Black colleges like Shaw University, Atlanta University, Virginia Union University, Fisk University, Morehouse College, Howard University, Talladega College, and Clark College, to name a few. The political enfranchisement of these newly freed Blacks was on the verge of becoming a reality during this period as personified in the presence of two black United States Senators and a Black governor of the state of Louisiana.

Contrary to some accounts, the period of Reconstruction cannot be dismissed simply as a period of carpetbaggers and political chicanery. It was America's first attempt to truly live consonant with its highest ideals as ensconced in the Declaration of Independence—that is to say that we are all "created equal and endowed by our creator with certain inalienable rights." As America embraced some of the basic tenets of its democracy, tangible benefits resulted for Whites as well as Blacks. Historian Lerone Bennett, Jr., in his book *Before the Mayflower: A History of the Negro in America, 1619–1964,* summarizes well the significance of this period for the soul and sinew of America:

Never before had the sun shone so bright. . . . Negroes and whites were going to school together, riding on street cars together and cohabitating, in and out of wedlock (Negro men were marrying white women in the South, but it was more fashionable, investigators reported, for white men to marry Negro women). An interracial board was running the University of South Carolina where a Negro professor, Richard T. Greener, was teaching white and black youth metaphysics and logic.

In Columbia, South Carolina, men were sampling democracy and finding it to their liking. The fabulous Rollins sisters—three *cafe au lait* descendants of a Negro-white union—were operating a Paris-type salon for movers and shakers and hostile critics were saying that more legislation was passed there than in the legislature. On hot nights, Negroes and whites walked the wide streets arm in arm and went perhaps to Fine's Saloon for a cold drink. The social life was gay, glittering, and interracial.[1]

In terms of politics and social appearance, relations between the former slaves and former slave owners were a reflection of the ideal of American democracy. There was substance behind the symbols of equality, justice, and good government. Again, Bennett's commentary on the period is insightful:

When the constitutional conventions [that were held in the South after the Civil War] met, some Southerners again put their heads into the sand. Surely "Sambo" would make a fool out of himself. After all, what did he know about the whereases and therefores of Anglo-Saxon government? Again the South was disappointed. The constitutions were excellent documents. They were so good, in fact, that some states were content to live under them for several years after the Democrats regained power.

The constitutions were not entirely the work of Negroes. The much-maligned "carpetbaggers" (Northern-born white men) and "scalawags" (white Southerners) were dominant elements in all of the conventions. But Negroes played important roles, especially in the Big Three—South Carolina, Louisiana and Mississippi.

South Carolina's Constitution, like most Reconstruction constitutions, made the state a much more positive force in the lives of the peoples. It eradicated every form of slavery, abolished imprisonment for debt, authorized universal male suffrage and gave the state its first divorce law. White women and poor white Southerners, it should be remembered, were emancipated with the slaves.

Negro delegates were largely responsible for the most important innovation in Reconstruction governments—the establishment of a public school system for poor and rich, black and white. In Mississippi, Louisiana, and South Carolina, incidentally, the laws called for interracial school systems.[2]

The period of Reconstruction might not have been Shangri-la; but in terms of good government, it was a lot better than what preceded it.

In 1876, all of the promise and potential that the Reconstruction period represented was lost. With the end of that era, the nation went from appropriating the highest ideals in its politics to apostasy, from the politics of inclusion and parity to the equivalent of apartheid American-style. The wholesale disenfranchisement of Blacks through terror and intimidation became the order of the day. The ethos of the era marking the end of Reconstruction was the "Blacks had no rights Whites were bound to respect." It was the decision of the Dred Scott case in 1857 revisited.

The disenfranchisement that became commonplace in 1876 became "common law" in 1896 with the *Plessy v. Ferguson* Supreme Court decision. The substance of the decision was that while states could not discriminate, individuals could. So, "separate but equal" along lines of color became the law; separate and unequal along lines of color

46

became the reality. The *Plessy* decision would prove devastating to the cause of democracy, justice, and community. In heart-rending fashion Bennett details the tragedy:

> Brick by brick, bill by bill, fear by fear, the wall grew taller and taller. . . . White nurses were forbidden to treat Negro males. White teachers were forbidden to teach Negro students. South Carolina forbade Negro and white cotton mill workers to look out the same window. Florida required "Negro" textbooks and "white" textbooks to be segregated in warehouses. Oklahoma required "separate but equal" telephone booths. New Orleans segregated Negro and white prostitutes. Atlanta provided Jim Crow Bibles for Negro and white witnesses. . . .
>
> By "grandfather clauses," literacy and understanding tests and white primaries, the Negro was excluded from the electorate. "Pitchfork" Ben Tillman, the South Carolina demagogue, said, "We have done our level best; we have scratched our heads to find out how we could eliminate the last one of them. We stuffed ballot boxes. We shot them [Negroes]. We are not ashamed of it."
>
> These devices were extremely effective. In 1896, for example, there were 130,344 Negro voters in Louisiana. . . . In 1900, two years after adoption of a state constitution with a "grandfather clause," the 5,320 Negro voters were a minuscule minority in every county. . . .
>
> In the peak years of the Terrible Nineties, which Rayford Logan has called the low point of the Negro's status in America, a Negro was lynched somewhere every two days or so. Lynching became in C. S. Johnson's words "a hybrid of sport-vengeance," became in Myrdal's words a form of "witch-hunting," became in H. L. Mencken's words a diversion which often took "the place of the merry-go-round, the theatre, the symphony orchestra, and other diversions common to larger communities." Newspapers advertised lynchings in advance. Crowds came from afar on chartered trains. . . .
>
> [Contrary to common perception] only a small percentage

of the Negroes who died by the rope or in burning fires were accused of rape. Others were charged with testifying against whites in court, seeking another job, using offensive language, failing to say "Mister" to a white man, disputing over the price of blackberries, attempting to vote, accepting a job as postmaster and being too prosperous.[3]

Lock, stock, and barrel, Blacks were sold down the river, in some ways literally as well as figuratively. This could not have happened without the support of the Constitution and some rather esteemed American institutions—particularly most major White religious denominations. Their complicity with "powers and principalities" bent on legal, political, and social disenfranchisement of Blacks, and subsequently poor Whites, was a sin of omission and commission. Most major denominations had struggled to the point of schism over the issue of slavery. During the post-Reconstruction period, the near reenslavement of Blacks was an issue about which these same Churches were for the most part silent; and that silence was deafening and defeating to the causes of democracy, decency, and human dignity.

Against this backdrop the drama of the Civil Rights Movement was played out. Not just were details of the law changed, but the tenor of the times was turned inside out. The Civil Rights Movement was a bright day not only for the democratic process, but also for human dignity. When George H. White, the last Black Congressman of the post-Reconstruction period, bid adieu to his congressional colleagues in 1901 he said, "This is perhaps the Negroes' temporary farewell to the American congress; but let me say, Phoenix-like he will rise up some day and come again."

The Civil Rights Movement stirred the ashes. Blacks returned to the Congress. They returned to the city halls and state houses of the South and achieved newfound political prominence in the North and in the heartland of America.

As important as the political victories was the extent to which hope came alive for Blacks and their spirits soared to new heights. It was a powerful Movement. And, like the period of Reconstruction before it, it was the impetus for freedom for a lot of other people—women, Hispanics, gays and lesbians. The Civil Rights Movement ushered in an era in which Americans began to entertain the notion that maybe the lion could lie down with the lamb and that we didn't have to "study war no mo'." It was a time of profound change, and the church was the principal change agent.

While a number of individuals took issue with the order of the day during the post-Reconstruction period, only one institution had as its raison d'être the abnegation of the negation of Black people in America. That institution was the Black church. The Black church sowed the seeds of equal worth and a holistic vision of human community during the dark and difficult years after Reconstruction. It was no wonder then that it was there to reap the fruits on that now famous day in 1955 in Montgomery, Alabama, when Rosa Parks refused to give up her seat on the bus and appealed to her pastor and church for help.

The Movement as Church History

Most analysts of the Civil Rights Movement treat it as a significant event in the political history of this nation. But much is obscured in terms of the how, why, and what the Movement represented if it is not viewed as a progeny of the church—the Black church.

Despite the fact that other individuals and institutions attempted to act as advocates for the rights of Blacks and

49

other disenfranchised in American society, only one institution could have done so effectively in 1955—the Black church. Only the Black church had the power (numbers) and the purpose (vision). To appreciate what I mean, Cornel West's definition of the Black church is helpful:

> The black church—a shorthand rubric that refers to black Christian communities of various denominations that came into being when African-American slaves decided, often at the risk of life and limb, to "make Jesus their choice" and to share with one another their common Christian sense of purpose and Christian understanding of their circumstances—is unique in American culture. This is so because it is the major institution created, sustained, and controlled by black people themselves; that is, it is the most visible and salient cultural product of black people in the United States. The profound insights *and* petty blindnesses, immeasurable depths *and* immobilizing defaults, incalculable richness *and* parochial impoverishment of that complex hybrid people called Afro-Americans surface most clearly in the black church.[4]

Because the Black church was what it was, the Movement could become what it would be. A primary focus of the Black church was (and is) the definition of the African American story; and the redefinition of history. Its fundamental statement was that Blacks were somebody in the demographics of the divine, not simply "strangers in a strange land" as characterized by this culture.

Illustrative of this point is the impact of the Black church on Martin Luther King Jr., the titular head of the Civil Rights Movement. Cornel West, in an address titled "Martin Luther King, Jr.: Prophetic Christian as Organic Intellectual," rightly roots Martin's moral acumen in the Black church. He states, "The broad black Christian worldview that King heard and adopted at his father's church [was a] worldview [that] put the pressing and urgent problem of evil—the utterly and undeniably *tragic* character of life and history—at its center. . . . Its emphasis was on survival and struggle in the face of an alternative of absurdity and insanity."[5] This worldview became the Zeitgeist of an age.

Given this orientation of the church, and the masses under its influence, it is no wonder that on December 5, 1955, when Rosa Parks decided to defy the law and not give up her seat to a White man, she turned to her church. The church—the Black church—responded. It became God's prophetic instrument for the hour. It is important to note that the initial response was not meant to start a movement; it was simply a response to the moment. Yet, it was one of the church's finest hours.

It was the principal spawning ground for leadership in the Movement—both lay and clergy. The Fannie Lou Hamers and the Dorothy Cottons of the Movement were churchfolk. The generals in the Lord's army were Martin Luther King Jr., Joseph Lowery, Ralph Abernathy, Major J. Jones, and Andrew Young, the list is legion. But the charge these churchfolk led was not simply the symbols they employed—which were clearly in keeping with the tradition of the Black church. The leadership of the Movement acted on the weight of their moral authority to leverage the change they sought. They saw themselves as the church in action. The Reverend Joseph E. Lowery, a founder and current president of the Southern Christian Leadership Conference, recalls a meeting with arch-segregationist, former Alabama Governor Wallace.

I told him, "I don't come here as a civil rights leader. I come as a Methodist pastor to a Methodist layman. God's going to hold you accountable." Surprised, Mr. Wallace objected. . . . He said, "Well, I'm not doing anything." I said, "Yes you are. You're inflaming people. You caused [civil rights worker] Viola Luizzo's death. You get on television raving and ranting." Wallace was never the same after that. Always after that he attacked the federal government. He didn't attack blacks.[6]

Beyond being a spawning ground for leadership, the passion and power of the Movement was religious. The stamp of the church on the Movement was evidenced in the music, which was the metronome to which folks marched, protested, sat-in and prayed-in. Those songs— renditions of old Negro spirituals—not only set the mood for the Movement, they also reflected the mind of the Movement. These "church" songs were not secularized or sanitized for Movement use. The theological and ethical tenets contained in these songs were accentuated. Freedom and justice were the meanings of the songs, and freedom and justice were the messages of the Movement.

The point being made in the spiritual "Oh, Freedom" is clear:

> Oh, freedom! Oh, freedom!
> Oh, freedom all over me!
> An' befo' I'd be a slave,
> I'll be buried in my grave,
> An' go home to my Lord an' be free.

Freedom is ascribed an ultimate value, God sanctions a freedom agenda, and ultimate vindication is the reward for those who work toward freedom's goal. Though such songs were obviously religious and forged in the crucible of slavery, they provided a language that gave insight and inspiration to push forward a contemporary political agenda. The use of these songs not only indicated the historical nature of the freedom struggle, but they also commented on how the Movement understood itself. The spirituals were religious songs, and this was a religious movement.

The voices of the Movement were those of churchfolk. What they said and sang came from the pulpit and pews, but the ultimate statement of the religious roots of the Movement was reflected in the vision.

The vision of the Movement was painted using religious imagery, and the values were religious as well. Again and again, those values came through as new milestones were negotiated, and the troops were inspired to action. The vision and values were most evident in the words of Martin Luther King Jr., as he called America to conscience and to move in making "justice a reality for all God's children" and chided allies in this mission to respond to physical force against this mission with "soul force."

It was clear, in both his preachments and prose, that Martin believed God was calling both Black and White Americans to examine their consciences about the state of race relations and justice in America. In examining Martin's thoughts, three threads held his "systematic" together: (1) an understanding of providence, (2) a humble sense of his own pastoral power, and (3) a deep commitment to an understanding of the role of the prophet as a "drum major for righteousness."[7]

These religious premises for Martin's thought were just as clearly premises for the Movement.

While, to a great extent, the goals of the Movement were couched in the words of one living person—Martin—the language of the Movement was the language of biblical prophets. After all, the freedom being sought could only

53

be talked about in a theological sense; in a constitutional sense the freedom of Blacks was nonexistent.

Rosa Parks precipitated the Movement and Blacks and others carried it on by assuming a "posture of freedom," that they understood as a God-given right versus a constitutional right. No one more precisely describes this phenomenon and concept than the late M. J. Jones in his book *Christian Ethics for a Black Theology.* He wrote:

> An adequate assumed posture of freedom must . . . express a sense of inner freedom that is a manifestation of what man has as an inner aim and what he must have for his future fulfillment as a person. . . .
>
> Such a positive freedom assumption opens up the fruitful possibilities that would have otherwise remained hidden if not seen by such positive anticipations. . . .
>
> Such an assumption is . . . claimed by a person who will not allow who he is, and what he may become, to be determined by the present evil world; rather, his being will be determined by the vision that has grown out of common personal and collective longings and higher personal and collective aspirations.
>
> Such a call for a new type of black person is a call for a new inner spirit which will refuse to let the creative act of a new assumption be dissolved away in immediate sense experiences.[8]

While Jones writes about this notion in a futuristic sense, it is possible to talk about it in the past tense. When Rosa Parks refused to give up her seat on the bus and to seek more rest for her soul than for her feet, she became free. Her freedom transcended anything that could be understood politically; it was a freedom that could only be interpreted theologically. She, and those she personified, saw beyond themselves in the present and became at that

moment what they saw for themselves in the future. That
which had only been talked about in eschatological terms
became the existential reality. Hope happened! Future
freedom could be embraced in the present because it was
a God-right. It was not necessary to wait for legislation for
something God ordained at creation.

The soul and sensibilities of the Movement were rooted
in how the church understood itself and history—tempo-
rally and eternally. This is why it is appropriate to talk about
the Movement as church history. What the Black church
precipitated with the Civil Rights Movement was not the
politicalization of religion, it was the transfiguration of
politics. The Black church, through the Movement, understood the dignity and depravity of persons, and ventured
forward based on the conviction that individuals and society could change and be changed to conform to the requirements of the Christian gospel: that justice, equality,
and harmony could replace order, universality, and peace
as the moral underpinnings of the sociopolitical order.

The Movement as a Monument
to a New Moral Order

The Civil Rights Movement represented a profound
break with the "traditional" politics of the period, and it
represented an equally profound embodiment of the principles of our democracy and the fundamental values of
Christian Populism. The significance of the Civil Rights
Movement is also reflected in the number of other movements it spawned and the permanence of the change it
wrought. It changed the configuration of politics along
color, class, gender, and generational lines; and it changed

the litmus test for electability and respectability for politicians from the local to the national level.

The tenor of the period was a commitment to justice for those historically excluded from the mainstream of rights and opportunities. This is not to say that these values were embraced by everyone; it is to say that these values had impact everywhere. The primary question asked in policy deliberations of every kind—social, legal, political—was, "Is it fair to the least of those in our midst?" At the inception of the Movement the definition of the least of those was considered in terms of race.

Even after the secularization of the Movement, with the ascendance of nonchurch leadership during this period of social change, the values that were the initial underpinnings of the Movement continued to dominate.

When the second phase of the Movement began with the Mississippi Freedom March in June 1966—when Stokely Carmichael advanced the slogan "Black Power" as the rallying cry—there was a battle over strategy, but the goals of freedom and justice remained the same. Despite the emergence of a more radical leadership in Huey P. Newton, Eldridge Cleaver, and H. Rap Brown—who had no objection to the use of violence—the virtues of justice and freedom were still valued. Even among the White radical left, the underlying premises—though couched in terms of a new world order—were consonant with the early aims of the Movement.

Though many remember the late '60s as a period of alienation and confrontation, it was more so a time of passion, purpose, and positive change. It was more than a time of long hair and rumpled clothes, free love and psychedelic trips. It was a period defined less by the Fifth

Dimension's "Age of Aquarius" than by Marvin Gaye's "What's Going On?"

The late '60s was a period when a generation of Americans, who had been raised to believe that America was supposed to be about justice, equality, and fair play, rose up in righteous indignation at the violation of these values. Southern police clubbing people who were praying, attack dogs biting people as they sang, hooligans bombing people at worship—simply because they were Black—offended the sensibilities of a generation, and they took the offensive against the brutality and subterfuge that violated their sense of what America was called to be.

For this generation, democracy for all Americans was essential to the integrity of the political system; and opportunity for all Americans was essential to the integrity of the economic system. In both regards much was lacking, and this generation took as its personal calling the politics of justice and equality. This was a time in which there was a belief that ordinary folk, through the power of protest and picket lines, could be a force for change. It was a time in which people were prepared to risk being "unrespectable" and to do battle for beliefs that edified all, rather than maintained individual comfort. The attitudes and actions of the times reflected the spirit of the Movement, even after the Movement's "spirit" had been forsaken.

Aside from establishing the Zeitgeist of an era, the Civil Rights Movement raised the stakes for the church in terms of missional credibility; in politics it raised the stakes for legitimacy and electability.

With the advent of the Movement, the church—Black and White—would never be the same. Within the Black religious community, Black theology was the dialectical response to the theology of the Movement. In addition,

Black theology created room for other theologies (feminist, Latin, liberation, and so on) in formal theological discourse.

While James Cone, the father of the modern Black Theology Movement, did not see Black theology as contradistinctive to the Movement by design, in fact it was. Yet, Black theology clarified—in theological terms—some of the basic tenets of the theology of the Movement, as well as arguing propositions in contrast. Using the theological tools of Euro-American systematic theology, Black theology illumined the theology implicit in the Movement's politics:

> King preached black liberation in the light of Jesus
> Christ and thus aroused the spirit of freedom among black
> people. . . . Black Theology [was built] on the foundation
> laid by King recognizing the theological character of the
> black community, a community whose being is inseparable
> from liberation through Jesus Christ.[9]

The norm for Black theology was (and is) the liberation of Black people and the revelation of Jesus Christ; this was, more or less, the major supposition of the Movement. While there was some correspondence between Black theology and the theology of the Movement, there was also contention: "Black Theology . . . [avoided telling] black people that love means turning the other cheek; that the only way to win your political freedom is through nonviolence."[10]

Despite the fact that there were points of contrast between Black theology and the theology of Martin and the Movement, my point is that without the Civil Rights Movement, the Black Theology Movement and the other movements would not have had the currency or impact that they had. They flourished as part of the legacy of the Civil Rights Movement.

But the most enduring testament to the reach of the Civil Rights Movement is in the area of politics. More than three decades later, progress still occurs as a result of the Movement's momentum. We see it in the increasing numbers of Black, female, and Hispanic elected officials. We see the progress reflected in the diversity in political appointments and in the policies that ensure diversity in the political life of our nation.

When we consider the increase in the number of minority and female officeholders in this country against the backdrop of discrimination some thirty years ago, we can only be inspired to go farther. This is not to suggest that we have progressed to the point at which we need to be; but neither should we be frustrated because we've failed to achieve all that we want.

In 1964, there were four Blacks in the United States Congress; in 1995, there are forty-one, and Representative John Lewis (D-Ga.) is the fifth-ranking member on the Democratic leadership team in Congress. While there is only one Black person (Carol Moseley-Braun) elected to the Senate since the defeat of Ed Brooke in 1978, the list of women in the Senate continues to grow longer.

As significant as the gains have been in the Congress, the most dramatic gains have been at the local level. The mayors of many of our major cities over the past thirty years have been Black, female, or Hispanic. A partial list of the cities includes Chicago, Los Angeles, Denver, Houston, Atlanta, and even "Bloody" Birmingham. In terms of electoral politics, there has been probably no symbol more profound of the Movement's impact on politics than the presidential candidacies of Jesse Jackson, one of Martin

Luther King Jr.'s disciples. His was one of the more viable presidential campaigns in modern political history. In 1984, the Jackson candidacy claimed 20 percent of its vote from the White community, which was unthinkable in light of the fact that the right of Blacks to vote had only been guaranteed for about twenty years. In addition, the Jackson candidacy resulted in the election of more Black delegates to the Democratic convention than ever before in the history of the party.

The Movement has also influenced the litmus test for electing White male politicians. Anyone running for public office these days must display a commitment to inclusive appointments and policies in order to get elected. Even in a city like Boston, where Blacks and Hispanics are a political minority, a reputation for racism endures; political credibility hinges on whether candidates can make the city work for everyone. In the 1983 mayoral campaign, the ability to make Boston an inclusive city was *the* test for legitimacy in that race.

One of the more humorous incidents that affirmed this very serious matter occurred at a mayoral forum on civil rights, which was held at my church. One of the candidates was a former city councillor from the predominantly Italian section of the city. While he was not a race-baiting politician, neither was he a paragon of liberal enlightenment. During the forum one of the panelists asked the candidates a question about the lack of equal access to housing. In a mostly Black audience, this man began his answer to the question by saying, "Let's call a spade a spade." The audience began to laugh because he was obviously oblivious to the fact that "spade" was a derogatory term for Black people. People laughed even more as he tried to chide them for what seemed to him a lack of appreciation for the seriousness of this matter. The need for an inclusive political agenda had become so much a part of the fabric of our political life that someone like this mayoral candidate had to struggle—however awkwardly—to embrace this ideal as central to his concerns.

So ensconced is this ideal of inclusiveness today that President George Bush might well have had one of the most inclusive cabinets in the history of our democracy. Though they obviously shared his views on many things, he had seen it necessary to bring minorities and women into the highest decision-making loop in our country just thirty years after apartheid American-style.

We have not yet seen the perfection of justice in our time, but the principles for its perfection have been established. The precedent for new standards, different political configurations, and the redistribution of political power has been set; this is why it is accurate to talk about the Civil Rights Movement as a monument to change. And, because the Movement had its genesis in the church and got much of its "juice" from the church, it is equally accurate to talk about the Civil Rights Movement as an epoch in church history.

THE POLITICAL CHURCH IN THE POST-MARTIN ERA

In his now famous "I Have a Dream" speech, Martin Luther King Jr., offered a vision of America as a beloved community in which reconciliation was real and justice and opportunity were the order of the day. While we have not yet reached the idyllic state, America is now very different from what it was when he offered this vision—and in some ways it approximates the vision.

Obviously, absolute equality does not exist; but there is a framework for its pursuit. We have the Civil Rights Act of 1964; not only are Blacks no longer relegated to the back of the bus, Blacks are executives in bus companies. We have the Voting Rights Act of 1965. I credit the Voting Rights Act with the unprecedented numbers of African Americans, women, and openly gay and lesbian persons who serve in Congress, act as governors, and run cities.

We have Executive Order 11246, issued in 1964, which calls for affirmative action to be taken in the hiring of minorities. In 1960 only 18 percent of Black families were middle class; by 1990 that number had increased to 42 percent.

In addition to the specific policy changes, the political dynamic from the 1960s to the 1990s is different. A set of metaphors that I have found helpful in distinguishing the political situation in the 1990s from the political situation in the 1960s is that in the '60s we were *pioneers,* and in the '90s we are called upon to be *settlers.*

During the Civil Rights Movement, our charge was to lead the nation to a place it had not been before. That place was dramatically detailed by the era's dominant figure—Martin Luther King Jr.:

> This nation will rise up and live out the true meaning of its creed. We hold these truths to be self evident, that all men are created equal . . . (and) sons of former slaves and sons of former slave-owners will be able to sit down together at the table of brotherhood . . . (and) even the state of Mississippi, a state sweltering with the heat of oppression, will be transformed into an oasis of freedom and justice.[1]

Our charge in this post-Martin era is to settle this land we have seen through the eyes of Martin and to build upon it using the tools made available because of the Movement. The legal, political, and social landmarks for this land of freedom and justice have been posted. African Americans, women, and other minorities have been guaranteed the right to vote. That right must be exercised to elect or reject politicians based on their commitment to get us to the promised land of justice and equality.

Though we have seen a burgeoning underclass over the past three decades, the minority community has also experienced a growing middle class. What this means is that the problem today is not defined solely in terms of race; another variable is class.

Because of the success of the Movement, more college-trained minorities and women than ever before have the experience and expertise to influence and make policy that can improve the plight of the least of those in our midst.

The church played a critical role in leading the nation to this point; therefore, it has an obligation to continue to move the nation forward. This means involving those who have benefited from the gains of the '60s in the move for change in the '90s. The church must engage its members in the process of change and be a source of inspiration for those outside the church to work for beliefs more noble than mergers and buyouts.

The generation that was on the cutting edge of change in the '60s is now on the cusp of leadership in business, government, and civic affairs. Young Blacks and Whites of the Movement years, who saw themselves as outsiders calling for something new, are now middle-aged and on the inside with the power to do that "new thing." The passion and perspective they held must be given new expression and interpretation into policies and programs. The logical question relative to the church and politics is, "What is the role of the political church in the post-Martin era?"

The mission of the church today is different from that of its predecessor of the '60s. For the pioneers of the '60s, the mission was to initiate. For the settlers of the '90s, it is to institutionalize. For the pioneers, life was making head-lines; for the settlers it is making headway. For the pioneers of yesterday the challenge was discrimination—color made you an outcast. For the settlers today, the challenges are about rescuing the underclass and saving the middle class. This problem of the lack of economic opportunity has a disproportionate impact along color, gender, and generational lines as did the problems of political, social, and legal options in the '60s. What I have been trying to describe in using the metaphor of pioneers versus settlers

James Hardaway

is the difference between being at center stage in the arena of protest politics versus occupying the stage in the arena of politics and policy. Again, it is the latter role that the church is called to play on the stage of current affairs.

In this post-Martin era I see the church being faced with three fundamental tasks. First, given the success of the Civil Rights Movement in opening up the body politic, the church's role in politics can (and must) extend beyond protests and pickets to policy and programs. (This shift also has implications as to who gets elected.) Given this call to political engagement, a basic question for the church, to paraphrase a biblical maxim, is, "How do we operate *in* the political world without becoming *of* the political world?" Or, to say it differently, "How should the church approach politics so that it does not get co-opted by the powers that be?"

A second task facing the church is protecting past victories. There are some clear indicators that while "Jim Crow" is dead "Jim Crow, Esq." is alive. Given the incidents of discrimination that still take place, it is clear that we have a way to go before Americans are judged by the content of their character rather than the color of their skin.

A third task is offering a relevant contemporary vision that is consistent with the basic tenets of Christian Populism. Fleshing out these tasks will be the focus of the remainder of this chapter.

The Church and Nonpartisanship

The first political task of the church in the post-Martin era is to participate in the political process without becoming co-opted. In the simplest words this means that the church (or churchfolk) must not become so partisan in its politics that it obscures the principles for which we stand. By definition this posture puts us in a position in the political process where we stand in prophetic judgment of that which takes place in the political arena, and we stand under judgment as we participate in the political process.

The prophetic voices of Ezekiel and Isaiah established a framework for a moral voice that "checks and balances" principalities and powers with political authority. The church today assumes this role; to restate a point already made, the role of the church is to enhance the possibilities for justice. Assuming this prophetic role should not be interpreted to mean that the church should stand on the sidelines and preach *at* the political establishment. Being nonpartisan doesn't mean that churchfolk have to dissociate themselves from political parties. Quite the contrary is the case.

The wheels of governance in a democracy turn on the discussion of the platforms of candidates and policies and programs. We are required to get involved in the fray and "mix it up." Yet, with the priority the church must give to justice and opportunity, we cannot get caught up in the game of power for its own sake as institutionalized in political parties. We can never forsake our principles for party or position. Yes, we must participate in the discussions and debates about governance at every level. Sometimes that participation must be with a prophet's scorn, and other times with a Christlike tenderness. Sometimes it must be with the aim to break up; at other times to heal. But underlying our actions must always be the determination to be able to get up from the table with our integrity intact.

This nonpartisan perspective is, in essence, a stand against the *sanctification of power.* What I mean by the sanctification of power is ascribing to power the ultimate value as a good, in and of itself. It is to view power as an end rather than as a means to effect an end—such as the just society that is the aim of Christian Populism. Such a view of power values the state, a political party, and even the church as means to acquire power.

The church must take a stand against the sanctification of power for several reasons:

First, when the state, a political party, or the church is viewed as a means to power, it in effect becomes an object of power. The result is investing those institutions with ultimate authority, ascribing to them a level of perfection that is pretentious, to say the least. No institution is perfect in judgment or action.

A second problem created by the sanctification of power is that it fosters inappropriate expectations for allegiance and action. People who ascribe unwarranted authority to institutions respond to the actions of those institutions with statements and actions like "my country, right or wrong." If Rosa Parks had ascribed absolute authority to the state, she would not have taken the proactive step she did in declaration of her freedom. At the moment of decision, that which was moral superseded that which was legal. Implicit in her action was the understanding that governments by definition are imperfect and prone to error. Her status under government was in conflict with her status under God. Her greater sense of herself prevailed, and that is the point: no earthly institution is so mysterious and omnipotent that it is due blind commitment. Any institution, political or religious, is more accountable to its constituency when it functions under this sort of scrutiny.

If the state is to function well it must be subject to judgment. It has been said that "power has a way of corrupting absolutely." Understanding this, the church is called to argue against absolute allegiance—even to itself—in things political. As an earthly institution (though heavenly in aspiration) it too is imperfect and corruptible in nature. In fact the church, and particularly its spokespersons have done and said some things in the name of Jesus that I would suspect have made him wish that he had stayed on the cross. As the late Dr. M. J. Jones, former President of Gammon Theological Seminary, appropriately pointed out, whether one is discussing the Black church or White church, neither is without sin:

> Both the black and the white post–Civil War churches failed, in degrees and on many occasions, to become adequate instruments of God's calling to be a servant. . . . The white church allowed itself to become a tool of the cultural ethos; its theology attempted to justify slavery and to convert the black man to a belief that he was not equal to his white brother under God.
> The black post–Civil War church was not without its moments and occasions of sin. . . . It was poor; very often it became an object of paternalism and charity. But too often, to become such an object, it had to compromise both belief and action.[2]

The church has had its blighted moments. If the church is going to judge with integrity, it must stand to be judged. The church's fallibility is implicit in the present controversy about the role of religion in politics. No church, sect, or denomination can lay claim to the "truth" in a political context with its head in the sand or in the clouds. Political truths must reflect information and insights gleaned from a number of perspectives and positions. Because the church is an earthly institution, and thus imperfect, it cannot lay claim to absolute truth in a political context without correspondence with those of the political world. If the church is to call the political establishment to remove the speck from its eye, it must be prepared to remove the log from its own. If the judgment against institutional omnipotence is to be preached with integrity, the church cannot be guilty of committing the same sin. Conversely, those of the political world, because of their fallibility, cannot lay claim to ultimate truth while ignorant of the insight the church has to offer.

The effect of the church's stand against the sanctification of power is the affirmation of the integrity of other institutions and individuals that also strive to achieve and maintain a just and harmonious community. To glean an insight of the apostle Paul, though we are different parts, we are of one body, and every part is equally important to the life of that body if it is to be whole.

In preaching against the sanctification of power, the church affirms the sanctity of all and the subservience of none. In this way the church affirms that it is as important to the commonweal as any other political player. This approach enables the church to participate in the political process in such a way that it operates "*in* the political world without being *of* the political world."

Finally, the church must stand against the sanctification of power because it results in the unprincipled pursuit of power. Such a pursuit of power results in a degree of acrimony and incivility detrimental to the democratic process itself. In his book *The Confirmation Mess*, Stephen L. Carter offers an astute observation, relative to the political confirmation process, as to where this pursuit of power leads:

> Once (someone) decides to oppose a nominee, any argument will do. Nobody is interested in playing by a fair

Ends justify the way, means mentality

set of rules that supersede the cause of the moment; still less do many people seem to care how much right and left have come to resemble each other in the gleeful and reckless distortions that characterize the efforts to defeat challenged nominations. All that seems to matter is the end result: if the demonized nominee loses, all that has gone before is justified. Activists working against a nomination can say just about anything, and the news media will report it (as allegation, to be sure, or as fact), only worrying later about whether it was true.[3]

Carter's point relative to the confirmation process, and mine in general, is that the political process is defiled when the players feel the end (power) justifies the means. Our politics ought to be driven by a principled nonpartisanship rather than by nonprincipled partisanship. We need more statesmanship than gamesmanship. To insist on such is the first task of the church in the post-Martin era.

Securing Civil Rights Gains

The second task of the church in the post-Martin era is to protect those gains it helped to win, making America a more just and equitable country. A couple of areas deserving immediate attention are voting rights and affirmative action.

America is more just, and I dare say better, because of greater participation by African Americans and others brought into the political process as a result of the Voting Rights Act. Yet it is ironic that at a time when the world is witnessing the end of apartheid in South Africa, resulting in power sharing with Blacks, we are seeing a major act of power shearing taking place in the United States in the effort to dismantle Southern Black congressional districts.

70

The nation must be mobilized against this assault on justice. The church ought to be in the vanguard of this effort. In that same vein, given the drama of long lines of Black South African voters, some injunction to organize communities of color in the United States around a strategy of voter registration and mobilization should be initiated. The right to vote is being squandered because many, who have the most to gain, have lost focus on the connection between political participation and opportunity. As the church mobilized America's disenfranchised on their own behalf before, in order to secure the right to vote, it must organize them again in order to protect that right.

The other area in which the church must exercise some leadership in order to protect past gains is in the area of employment opportunity. In 1965, President Lyndon Johnson signed Executive Order 11246 mandating "affirmative action" as a way to ensure equal economic opportunity for minorities and women. At no time since then has affirmative action been under greater assault than it is right now! It is under assault philosophically by those who wrongly call it reverse discrimination. It is under assault politically, with the most organized effort now taking place in California by referendum—the California Civil Rights Initiative. And it is under assault legally and practically. The present Supreme Court has decided to take up the issue soon; and given the Court's present composition, we should be worried. On a daily basis, as companies downsize, the principles and policies of affirmative action are being violated as minorities disproportionately bear the burden of layoffs.

In the face of this assault in 1995, we do not need to turn back the clock to pre-1965. First of all, we need to protect affirmative action because it works! While it has not been a panacea that guarantees the full participation of all minorities and every woman in America's economic mainstream, it is clear that without it this nation would not have made the progress it has in becoming more fair and in providing greater opportunity for all. From 1960 to 1990 the percentage of African Americans in the workforce increased by 35 percent, the percentage of women increased by 23 percent, and the numbers for Hispanics and Asians were even more dramatic.

Second, although affirmative action has worked, it can hardly be said that because of it minorities and women have an unfair advantage in this economy. The reality is staggering in the face of the perception that affirmative action is reverse discrimination: African Americans and other minorities are still unemployed at almost twice the general rate and are paid a bit more than half as much when employed. Whites own thirty times more businesses than Blacks. Where is the unfair advantage Blacks and other minorities are supposed to hold?

The charge that affirmative action gives minorities and women an unfair advantage is fallacious on another front. It implies that every White male in the job market is better qualified than everyone else, that people should be able to get the exact jobs they want and when they want them, and that every minority has the job of his or her choice. Obviously, none of these things is true. The legitimate job crunch that Whites are feeling is not because of Blacks; Blacks are feeling it too. The problem is the downsizing of businesses and government, and the downsizing of paychecks that is occurring in many cases because of job displacement. The issue is, What does this nation do about this problem, while maintaining a commitment to the principles of fairness and opportunity for all?

72

Third, in a world marketplace defined by NAFTA and GATT, our diversity is a potential advantage that could clearly establish this nation as *the* leader in this new global economy. Affirmative action is one strategy to ensure that we harness that potential. The choice seems simple: we can continue to fight over our diminishing share of the global economic pie and watch the world pass us by; or we can utilize all the talent we possess across color, class, gender, and generation lines and thus compete and win. It is this second choice that the nation needs to make.

The assault on affirmative action is not simply an assault on fairness and opportunity for minorities and women; it is an assault on the future. The battle has been joined. It needs to be fought to ensure fairness and opportunity for all Americans, and to save the soul of this nation.

The church led the way in securing these gains; the church needs to lead the way in preserving them. This second task of the church is a defensive strategy. The third task is offensive, fashioning a new vision and agenda in light of a new reality.

A New Vision for a New Day

As I noted earlier, this country has improved significantly and dramatically in some very important ways over the last three decades; but all is still not right in America. In 1994, for the first time in U.S. history, this nation spent more per capita for criminal justice than for schools. In California, for example, twenty-eight prisons dot the landscape. They are as common as K Marts. Initially the state planned twelve new prisons by the end of the century. With the "three strikes, you're out" statute on the books, the state will need twenty new prisons by the end of the century and eighty in the next thirty years. The average cost per prisoner is $24,000 per year. George Washington University sociologist William Chambliss says of this phenomenon, "What we're seeing in the U.S. is a greater increase in the number of people in prison and a higher incidence of illiteracy. We are trading textbooks for prison cells." This is not the way things are supposed to be.

Our city streets are filled with far too many beggars, homeless and hungry families, and violent, errant children. If we are going to help those on the outside of the mainstream of American life, then they must be brought back into the mainstream of America's economic life. The church must lead the way in this effort.

Homelessness and hunger, and folks seeking handouts, are clearly economic problems; but I would also submit that drug abuse and youth violence are substantially economic problems as well. How can we convince young people that they ought not to take some drug-induced trip to fantasyland when their day-to-day reality is an economic nightmare? How can we convince them to turn from violence because life is precious, when they feel they have nothing to live for? Some argue the problems of drugs and violence result from parents having lost control of their kids. I counter, How can we expect many of these parents to control their kids when they've lost control of their own lives? People who have no place to work or no place to live feel *lost*.

To open up the economy and expand opportunity is the most compelling mission of the moment and the present charge and challenge of the church.

To accomplish this mission, we must fashion policies and programs to ensure adequate preparation (education), participation (employment), and parity (equity) for those who are left out. These are keys to enabling those mired in the economic swampland to swim in the economic mainstream.

Beyond fashioning the policies and programs for an inclusive economy, we must also deal with the deep racial divisions in America that represent a plague on our house.

In 1996, this nation will mark the one hundredth anniversary of the *Plessy v. Ferguson* Supreme Court decision. This decision gave constitutional credence to the notion of "separate but equal" and started this nation down the path to apartheid American-style. I believe we are moving perilously close to reliving this horrible episode of America's past. A 1994 study done by the National Council of Christians and Jews confirmed that today this nation is as divided along lines of race as it's ever been.

> We must overcome the racial divide which separates us. It is the morally right thing to do. We are all the same in the sight of God; herein lies the root of the injunction to "do unto others as you would have them do unto you." We must overcome our sense of division; the point is as clear as it is simple—"a house divided against itself cannot stand."[4]

Overcoming our sense of division is not only morally sound; it is also strategically sensible. If we are going to open up the economy and expand opportunity, we must forge a consensus that cuts across color, class, and community lines.

How soon we forget! One of the most profound examples of "revolutionary change" in this country was the Civil Rights Movement. A critical ingredient to the success of that Movement was the forging of a consensus in this nation based on the premise that discrimination against

Blacks was not simply a sin against African Americans, but that it threatened the very soul of America. If this nation is going to respond effectively to the clamoring and quiet desperation that so many in this country feel, we must reforge such a consensus. To do so means the principles of harmony and hope must be reflected in our morals and manners, and in the very way we attempt to mobilize people. Who bonds with the African American community—from inside and outside the community—is critical. Providing leadership for this multifaceted agenda of opportunity is the third task of the church.

I would not be so presumptuous as to suggest that this list of tasks is exhaustive of the political mission of the church in the post-Martin era; but I do believe it is indicative of the sort of things the church must do if it is to be appropriate for this moment.

FORGING A NEW POLITICAL CONSENSUS

I n chapter 3, I raised the issue of the need to address the deep racial divisions in America. In this chapter, I deal more substantially with how we came to be so divided, why we need to overcome the divisions, and how we can overcome them. While my emphasis is on racial divisions and discrimination in the United States, I also offer some observations about the issue of sexual discrimination. I do so because of the number of people affected by sexual discrimination and the primacy of this issue in the present national debate regarding discrimination in general.

The present fractured state of the nation had its beginnings in the demise of the Civil Rights Movement. Three concurrent political developments from that point onward precipitated the present state of affairs. First, other "freedom movements," inspired by the Civil Rights Movement and started as companions to it, became competitive movements. Second, generational and class divisions in the White community over Vietnam contributed to the general climate of acrimony and drained energy and vitality from the cause of civil rights and equal opportunity. Finally, those who were politically to the right of center exploited these tensions and pressed a political agenda that emphasized law and order over justice and opportunity. Let me flesh these statements out.

Initially the Civil Rights Movement stalled because the consensus about means and ends broke down. The end goal of the Movement was a more just and racially harmonious society; the means to that end was the process of working in harmony. The most profound yet simple statement of this belief was reflected in the anthem of the Civil Rights Movement: "We shall overcome . . . Black and White together . . . we shall overcome someday." By 1967, when America's cities were in flames, the level of anger over injustice had clearly reached a boiling point and the coalitions of the past were in jeopardy. Civil rights and racial harmony became secondary to the right to power, and power came to be perceived as being in conflict with partnership. We moved from "we shall overcome" to a series of power movements. Blacks organized. Women organized. Hispanics organized. Everybody organized as a means of defining themselves and developing separate justice agendas.

While it may have been important for everyone to have "a room of one's own," to borrow the title of Virginia Woolf's signature work, the effect was that America became a "house divided against itself." We came to see one another as competitors rather than as a community. The problem this presented was rather obvious; with the civil rights community fractured along color, class, gender, and generational lines, it was impossible to effectively challenge conditions that resulted in discrimination along color, class, gender, and generational lines. With the coalition unraveling, the consensus broke down, and progress was stymied.

The second current of discord that precipitated the end of the Civil Rights Era was the generational and class division in the White community that erupted over Vietnam. This schism was generational; those in power were of the World War II generation for whom it was unthinkable that the government would be challenged by its own citizens in a time of war. The schism was along class lines; it was primarily middle-class college students challenging America's role in Vietnam, and lower-class and working-class kids on the front lines in Vietnam defending America's role. There was a display no more dramatic of the estrangement in the United States over this issue than the confrontation at Kent State University. On May 4, 1970, the National Guard turned its guns on students protesting Vietnam; it seems as if on that day America also turned its back on idealism. Not only did students die in that confrontation, the consensus of what the United States should become died that day as well.

From the turbulence of those times arose another political force that moved this country to the right. Its titular head was Richard M. Nixon; the political mantra he used to meld a political base was that there was a "silent majority" longing for "law and order."

Two biblical metaphors are helpful in describing the political dynamic of that era. If the Civil Rights Era could be thought of as the Pentecost, then the post–Civil Rights Era was Babel. In the first period everyone talked to everyone else in a language and about an agenda that everyone seemed to understand. In the second period, no one seemed to understand anyone, and in such an environment it is not difficult to appreciate how a call for law and order might have had a certain appeal.

79

We didn't get law and order; at best it was the stifling of protest and the isolation of dissent. A generation of politicians forged pluralities based on the lowest common denominator rather than the common good. "Wedge issues" became a part of our political lexicon and typified the political strategies of choice.

Continuing along this path, the political arena has become a battleground instead of a place to discuss and debate legitimate differences of opinion. Campaigns have typically become nasty and negative. Even the confirmation of cabinet officers and judges, which at one point in history was like a stroll through the park for the nominee, is now more like a run for survival through a minefield. The continuing extent of estrangement and lack of consensus was reflected in the 1992 presidential election. For the first time in the modern era a U.S. president was elected with less than a clear majority.

The present fractured state of the nation begs that we forge a new political consensus in this country that cuts across color, class, gender, and generational lines. In a phrase, we need a new political order reflecting the *politics of consensus.*

The politics of consensus is as much about ends as means. A common axiom in politics is that you have "no permanent friends, only permanent interests." A fundamental premise of Christian Populism is that the only way to ultimately address permanent interest is within the context of permanent friends. This means forging a community with shared values and a shared vision of hope and harmony, justice, and opportunity. This is the essence of the politics of consensus.

For the rest of this chapter I will define some of the basic tenets of the politics of consensus and share some of my experiences in attempting to forge such a political consensus.

Principles for the Politics of Consensus

The primary impediment to a new political consensus is the great divide that exists in the United States. Life in this country is a "tale of two cities." For some it is "the best of times" and for others it is "the worst of times," but many are not quite sure why. The goal for forging the consensus is overcoming this divide. Race is at the root of our problem, yet the dilemma is not as plain as black and white. As described in a *Newsweek* special report on race relations in America, the problem is obscured because "mercifully, America today is not the bitterly sundered dual society that the Riot Commission grimly foresaw. Nor is it King's promised land of racial amity. Rather, it is something uneasily between the two."[1]

One could argue that, in the past, when we talked about the great divide that had to be overcome, it was clearly a racial divide. Now, because of the explosive growth of the Black middle class, many would insist that the great divide is one of class. I would argue that it is irrelevant to debate which is the dominant issue. On the one hand, the problems of poverty disproportionately affect people of color; on the other hand, the problem of class and race won't be overcome unless we can forge a consensus that cuts across color, class, *and* community lines. A no more eloquent statement of this has been put forth than that by Jesse Jackson at the 1988 Democratic National Convention, where he used the metaphor of a quilt to describe the human condition and the content of our hope:

America is not a blanket, woven from one thread, one color, one cloth. When I was a child in South Carolina, and Momma couldn't afford a blanket, she didn't complain and we didn't freeze. Instead she took pieces of old cloth— patches—wool, silk, gaberdine, croker sack—only patches good enough to shine your shoes with. But they didn't stay that way long. With sturdy hands and strong cord, she sewed them together into a quilt, a thing of power, beauty and culture. Now we must build a quilt together.

Farmers, when you seek fair prices, you are right— but your patch isn't big enough. Workers, when you seek fair wages, you are right, but your patch isn't big enough. Women, when you seek comparable worth and pay equity, you are right—but your patch isn't big enough. Mothers, when you seek Head Start, prenatal care and day care, you are right—but your patch isn't big enough. Students, when you seek scholarships, you are right—but your patch isn't big enough.

Blacks and Hispanics, when we fight for civil rights, we are right—but our patch isn't big enough. Gays and lesbians, when you fight against discrimination and for a cure for AIDS you are right—but your patch isn't big enough. Conservatives and progressives, when you fight for what you believe, you are right but your patch isn't big enough.

But don't despair. When we bring the patches together, make a quilt, and turn to each other and not on each other, we the people will always win.[2]

This sentiment not only appropriately defines the present situation, it also underscores the power and potential of a populist agenda for the church based on the notion of a just and reconciled community. This reality of our interconnectedness and interdependence crystallizes, like no other, the mission and political agenda of the church. This agenda is one that the church has the language to talk about. The prophet Isaiah symbolized that agenda by the lion and the lamb lying down together. Dr. Samuel D.

Proctor, Professor Emeritus at Rutgers University, makes this same point using the message of the Gospels in his explanation of the good Samaritan story. He says:

> Jesus deliberately put a Samaritan in this story from among a great many candidates he might have chosen. . . . I wonder how spontaneous this was to choose a despised member of a mixed race. He must have intended to show that race and class had nothing to do with virtue and that genes and status had nothing to do with compassion. He meant to make all of us candidates for goodness.[3]

The apostle Paul also understood that agenda to be reflected in our oneness in Christ: "There is no longer Jew or Greek, there is no longer slave or free, there is no longer male or female; for all of you are one in Christ Jesus" (Gal. 3:28). The hymnist John Oxenham strikes a similar chord:

> In Christ there is no east or west,
> in him no south or north;
> but one great fellowship of love
> throughout the whole wide earth.[4]

The point is, the work of the church is to call us to "community," because by being in community so many other issues are resolved. To be a community requires embracing one another's hopes, sharing one another's pain, and claiming one another's cause. It requires working together for the realization of those hopes, the mediation of that pain, and the victory of those causes.

As we attempt to address the problems of poverty, disenfranchisement, and injustice, we must appreciate that they can be resolved only within the context of a reconciled community. Only when we—as members of the human family—come to fully appreciate that we must learn to live together as people of wisdom or perish apart as fools, will we treat this Christian Populist agenda with the kind of urgency it deserves. The church must provide the leadership in getting us all to the point of embracing this vision. To be a reconciled community is both the means and the end of political religion—that is, Christian Populism—and is fundamental to forging a political consensus in our time.

Experiences in Consensus Building

As I try to build bridges between the Black and Jewish communities and the Black and Hispanic communities, I employ some action steps. I call them the Ten Commandments of Consensus Building.

THE TEN COMMANDMENTS
OF CONSENSUS BUILDING

I. Thou must affirm the value of our diversity.
This perspective takes one step beyond the traditional view of America as a melting pot. More appropriate descriptions are former New York Mayor David Dinkins's metaphor of the community as a mosaic, or Jesse Jackson's metaphor of the community as a quilt.

II. Thou must know the history of the relationship; that is, the pitfalls and false starts.
An understanding of the history of the relationship and the players can help prevent the problem George Santayana noted: "Those who cannot remember the past are condemned to repeat it."

III. Thou shalt affirm not only the desirability of collaboration but also the necessity of collaboration.

84

IV. Thou shalt acknowledge the points of contention.

There must be an honest and open discussion of the areas around which there are real disagreements.

V. Thou shalt be sensitive to the other's pain and problems.

Though the realities might be similar, understanding the uniqueness of the respective histories is important to moving beyond posturing over whose ox has been gored the deepest.

VI. Thou shalt look for those things that are shared in common.

Blacks and Jews share a common history of slavery and an affinity for the liberation themes of the Old Testament and especially the Torah. Blacks and Hispanics share the experience of disproportional impoverishment and disenfranchisement. Women share the experience of the "glass ceiling" limiting employment promotion opportunities and the lack of job opportunities in general.

VII. Thou must deal with issues that are respectively important.

Only reciprocal benefits for the parties involved will make the effort of building a relationship worthwhile.

VIII. Thou shalt seek to involve and identify new leadership, not to compete with present leadership but to complete the circle of leadership.

It is important to involve people in the bridge-building process who don't bring old baggage and are able to see new possibilities.

IX. Thou must seize the opportunity for a breakthrough in reaching out.

For example, Clarence Thomas's confirmation hearings to the Supreme Court represented a real opportunity for men to reach out to women in order to address the problem of sexual harassment.

X. Thou shalt take the initiative to reach out even if there is no opportune time.

The following sections reflect each of these commandments, in varying combinations. In some cases they reflect lessons learned in my experiences and experiments in trying to bring communities together.

On Blacks and Hispanics

Even the casual observer of political, social, and economic events will note that many Blacks and Hispanics share similar lives—disproportionately high levels of poverty and unemployment, poor education, inadequate health care, and poor relations with police and other community authorities.

It is equally obvious that, up to this point, the Black and Hispanic communities have chosen not to give the necessary priority to joining together to improve their circumstances. The factors that have kept the two communities separate are formidable indeed.

First, because the country has gone through a period of austerity related to government spending, the two communities at times perceive one another as competitors for the same dwindling resources. Second, cultural differences (different languages, different religious practices) are sources of discord between the two communities. Third, the two communities have different levels of organization, sophistication, and expectations that may serve as points of contention. And finally, external forces seek to exacerbate every difference and dissension in order to undermine the potential power that would result from such a union.

While the impediments to Black-Hispanic unity are very real, attempts to lay the groundwork for some kind of unified program have been made. In 1980, I convened a conference at my church to attempt just that. The purpose of the conference, organized by and attended by leaders from Black and Hispanic communities throughout New England was twofold: to discuss the problems and prospects facing the two communities in the 1980s, and to discuss ways that the two might work together to forge a better future. A number of issues that were raised then are relevant even today.

For almost thirty years Blacks and Hispanics have been caught between the drive for affirmative action, on the one hand, and, resistance to any compensatory measures, on the other. Black and Hispanic representatives at that 1980 conference were united in their belief that only through coalition could past gains be protected and future gains ensured.

Two questions emerged immediately. The first was: Is a Black-Hispanic coalition a realistic prospect?

The conference participants were unanimous in their answer, and the answer was yes. The two communities have no choice. In the words of one participant: "Whether it's a wedding of love or a shotgun wedding, the marriage must take place." Together Blacks and Hispanics represent a formidable force. The possibility of the two communities being played off each other is significantly diminished, and the possibility of furthering the mutual agenda of remedy and parity is, accordingly, significantly increased.

The second question was: What can be expected from a Black-Hispanic alliance?

First, if the "marriage" is going to take place, there will have to be some opportunities for "courting." The very real points of tension between the two communities must be aired, acknowledged, and resolved. Second, participants agreed that there should be unified support of political involvement by both. The 1994 anti-immigrant referendum in California, Proposition 187, is an example of a political issue on which the two communities could unite. This proposal affects Hispanics and also Black immigrants, such as Haitians. Third, the two communities must together renew support for existing educational reform and for programs to address problems such as drug abuse.

There is a significant distance between the sentiment that the Black and Hispanic communities must form a coalition, and the reality of such an alliance. But the conference we held demonstrated the willingness to try, and the gap between the rhetoric and reality of a Black-Hispanic connection began to close.

On Blacks and Jews

From the days of my earliest involvement in the Movement I was aware of the historic connection between Blacks and Jews. I was equally aware of the "ups and downs" of that relationship in the post–Civil Rights Era. I was moved to try personally to effect a new relationship between our two communities on October 3, 1980. On that day a bomb exploded outside the Rue Copernic Synagogue in Paris. It was an explosion heard around the world, not because it precipitated an international crisis between sovereign states, but because this was the most dramatic attempt since World War II to kill Jews, no matter what their nationality.

Nowhere was the explosion heard more loudly than in Paris, where almost two hundred thousand Parisians of all political persuasions took to the streets to protest that despicable deed. But it was also heard in the Black community in the United States, for it sounded the common vulnerability of both communities. While the culprit(s) who planted the bomb certainly meant it for evil, it was another shock to the Jewish and Black communities in the United States. It caused some of us to seriously reexamine, and see the need to revitalize, a deteriorating age-old alliance.

Two months later, I journeyed to Israel and to Paris. I met with Jewish political and religious leaders to get a feel for how they understood the state of affairs in Israel and in the Jewish community in diaspora, and to sound out their opinions on what seemed to be a worldwide resurgence of racism. Three concerns dominated the discussions we had. Those concerns represented a recent history of the points of contention between African Americans and Jews, as well as the possibilities for reconciliation that exist for the two communities.

First, our assessment of the historic conflict between the Arabs and Israeli Jews was that it was, and is, a life-and-death issue, in two very real (not rhetorical) ways. One is the obvious geopolitical aspect of the problem, which relates to the very existence of Israel. The other is the moral dimension. Israel understands itself as a country that rests upon the foundations of liberty, justice, and peace. Thus, the conflict that persists—within and outside its borders—is anathema to Israel's very being. Therefore, finding a just and humane solution to the conflict is more important to Israel's survival than simply finding a military solution to the conflict.

Second, we were concerned about how to interpret the ambiguity reflected in the 1980 election of Ronald Reagan as president. The ambiguity arose from what seemed to be contradictory signals coming from the Reagan camp. On the one hand, there were commitments voiced by Reagan to give priority to the problems of the economy (namely, inflation and unemployment) and defense, both of which would seem to bode well for Blacks and Jews in the United States and in Israel. On the other hand were noises from the Reagan camp to the effect that the Voting Rights Act, desegregation, and so on, needed to be repealed.

Third, given the tenuous state of economies worldwide, and the historic inclination to scapegoat minorities as a diversion from inadequate economic policies, as well as the present resurgence of attitudes and acts of racism directed against the Black and Jewish communities, we felt it important that the historic relationship between the Black and Jewish communities be reexamined and revitalized in order to respond.

While these concerns suggested where the two communities should have been headed at the time, it did not negate the fact that there were some difficult and tricky political and moral waters to navigate. Problems of energy and economy relative to Israel, the issue of East-West hegemony in the Middle East, and the vulnerability of European Jewry from political elements on the Left that identify with the Palestinians, as well as political elements on the Right that are explicitly racist signaled anything but smooth sailing. Those attempting to wade through such issues as equity for Blacks in our economy and majority rule in South Africa also faced many quagmires.

Obviously, since that time there have been some very significant political changes. We have witnessed a historic peace accord between Israel and the Palestinians and freedom for Blacks in South Africa. Yet there were some lessons learned and principles gleaned from my earlier efforts at fencemending that are still relevant to Blacks and Jews coming together.

Four principles stood out as important to forging a bond between African Americans and Jewish Americans.

First, if Blacks and Jews are going to be in coalition with one another rather than in conflict, the two communities must affirm that they have more in common than in contention with one another. There is a theological kinship rooted in compatible faiths. And the two share a historical experience that has included a descent into the hell of slavery and ascent to the higher ground of freedom.

Despite what the press might have us believe, the two communities still share a common political outlook on many thorny issues. According to various polls, Blacks and Jews are in greater agreement on the issues of affirmative action and American support for Israel than any other two groups in America. Both tend overwhelmingly to support Democratic candidates, particularly at the presidential level. These commonalities need to be cultivated.

Second, if the relationship between these two communities is to be marked by harmony rather than cacophony, the points of contention between the two must be overcome. That may sound obvious, but for too many on both sides, it has been easy to "agree to disagree." That won't work. The differences become small sores that will not heal, and after enough scratching and picking, they begin to infect the entire relationship. For example, if Jews perceive Blacks as unconcerned about Israel's security and sovereignty, or if Blacks see the Jewish community as opposed to Black aspirations for a secure place in the economic mainstream, there won't be much of a basis for any relationship, or any need for one. The issues still unresolved are the issues on which agreement must be reached.

Third, if we are going to rebuild bridges, we must reach out and bring new people into the conversation. A lot has happened since we last really talked to one another. The Black community has gone from total political disenfranchisement to Black Power and Black separatism to significant mainstream Black political strength in many American cities. During the same period, the Jewish community has had to respond to the imperatives of several Mideast wars, a growing influence in world affairs, and a reemergence of anti-Semitism. The leaders who presided over these shifts in emphases undoubtedly intended to serve their respective communities well. But, perhaps they now need help in redirecting attention to a common agenda. New voices need to be heard. It is critical that those new voices reflect a new sensitivity.

On a trip to Israel in 1984, sponsored by the Anti-Defamation League, I visited Yad Vashem and felt the pain of the Holocaust. It made me more appreciative of why many in the Jewish community reacted with anger and protest to Jesse Jackson's reference to New York as Hymietown, and it was not accurate for Black leaders to characterize that reaction simply as racism or the desire to stifle Black political aspirations. The Black community needs leaders who handle such tense situations with sensitivity and restraint. Similarly, it is clear that many in the Jewish community did not appreciate what Jesse Jackson's presidential campaigns meant for Black people. Anyone who feels the pride in Israel as she stands up to a world that has forsaken her so many times should be able to imagine what Black people felt when Jackson stood tall; when he out-debated the other candidates on national TV; when Black boys and

92

girls began to dream for the first time that they might grow up to be president; when old folks raised under Jim Crow could speak with pride at his successes. These were proud moments for Black America. The Jewish community needs leaders who understand these aspirations, that pride, and can temper their concerns with sensitivity and restraint.

A fourth requirement for rebuilding the alliance between Blacks and Jews is that leaders from both camps must move beyond talk to action, on whatever scale. The benefits of coalition-building were brought home to me during a mission of Black and Jewish leaders to Israel in September 1987, which I co-led along with Leonard Zakim of the Anti-Defamation League. The purpose of the mission was to enable the Black participants to get a better feel for Israel's significance in the American Jewish community, and for everyone to share their respective concerns about issues that affect Black-Jewish relations. Upon returning home, our delegation learned that Israel had moved to impose new sanctions on South Africa and that the decision was expedited as a result of our meeting with Foreign Minister Shimon Peres and Political Director General Yossi Beilin.

We went without the intent or the authority to negotiate a change in foreign policy. Those of us from the Black community went as friends; the Jewish members of the delegation went as family. In that spirit we seized the opportunity to share with Foreign Minister Peres some heartfelt concerns of both the Black and the Jewish communities concerning apartheid and the relationship of nations around the world toward South Africa. In our meeting, we encouraged Israel to continue to accelerate its policy to not renew or enter into new military contracts with South Africa. In addition, we emphasized our hope that all the world's nations, including Israel, would completely sever economic ties with the South Africans.

As important as was the initiative taken by Israel against South Africa, equally important was the fact that Black and Jewish Americans *together* were raising the issue. Aside from the progress represented for Israel, the fact that the initiative was encouraged by a joint mission of Black and Jewish leaders had a positive impact on Black-Jewish relations. In addition, this sort of initiative is indicative of what is possible when a coalition works.

Blacks and Jews have much to say to one another and to do together. We need to beat back the demons of racism and anti-Semitism that haunt our personal and cultural memories. We need to reach out to new individuals and new institutions—not to circumvent past efforts, but to break an escalating cycle of misinformation, mistrust, and hyperbole. If we dare to defy the potential pitfalls, we can rebuild the bridges between our communities and chart a common political agenda.

On Sexual Discrimination

The issue of sexual harassment raised during the Supreme Court confirmation hearings for Clarence Thomas in 1991 dominated not only the airwaves, but also Americans' consciousness and conversation, as has no other quasi-political event I have witnessed.

The hearings also resulted in some unprecedented soul-searching by men and soul-baring by women. Despite this, I am concerned that we might be letting the opportunity prompted by the hearings pass without doing something about a serious problem, of which sexual harassment is basically a barometer.

The problem to which I'm referring is sexual discrimination, in the broadest sense. Women are more likely than men to live in poverty. Women make two-thirds the salary of men when similarly employed. Women have a glass ceiling to contend with in the corporate world, prohibiting promotion and advancement.

Once you get beyond the most blatant forms of harassment—touching, making lewd gestures, and the like—the line of demarcation is not as clear. It's not clear because we live in a culture in which every product, from granola to cars, is sold with sex. In matters of the heart, men are still expected to be the pursuers, and the more tenacious men are in the pursuit of the women of their dreams, the more romantic they are considered to be.

Our age is one of confusion about sexual roles and responsibilities. In a 1991 poll, 63 percent of women questioned said they would be insulted if propositioned by a coworker; 67 percent of men said they would be flattered.

While we continue to struggle with the complexity of the relationships between the sexes, we can tackle some rather objective issues that have profound implications relative to the issue of power, which sexual harassment is ultimately about.

First, we as a nation—and men in particular—need to confess that individually and culturally, we have subjected our mothers, sisters, wives, daughters, and female friends to dehumanizing, disrespectful, and insensitive behavior.

Second, we need to address some issues that affect the objective reality of discrimination in which women live. Let's address the issue of equal pay for equal work. Let Congress move to bring themselves under the law as it relates to discrimination, including Title VII. Finally, let's pass the Equal Rights Amendment to the Constitution.

The truly national debate that began with the Thomas hearings can take one of several turns. It can simply be another flash in the pan in the political discourse of this nation, dominating the political scene for a moment, only to find us rushing on to the next hot issue tomorrow. Or it can result in further polarization between the sexes. While this polarization won't be so extreme as to spell the end of romance, it could result in less camaraderie between women and men in the workplace. The most positive turn this debate could take would be to spark a new partnership that creates the conditions for the guilty to be redeemed and the violated to be restored.

Certainly, taking this issue seriously is a critical precondition to forging a new political consensus in this country.

Building a New Consensus

Do the bilateral concerns and efforts referred to earlier provide the groundwork for an expanded consensus? The short answer to that question is yes. They provide the potential, only if we interpret with the same skill and precision why and how it is urgent to move quickly to expand the consensus. To make the point somewhat differently, there is some value in pursuing coalitions on a bilateral basis—Blacks and Hispanics, Blacks and Jews, men and women. Aside from ends that can be achieved, the means to consensus are less encumbered because there are fewer issues to resolve than if we were attempting to build a consensus along multilateral lines. But as it is in physics, so it is in politics; everything with an upside has a downside. While there are fewer issues to resolve when building coalitions bilaterally, there is always the danger that the basis for the coalition will be an "us against them" mentality, which makes the ultimate goal of a multilateral consensus difficult, if not impossible.

If it is the politics of consensus we want—an agenda of hope and harmony, justice and opportunity—then we must coalesce across color, class, gender, and generational lines as we structure this new creation. The means is, in fact, the end in this effort.

While, as I pointed out earlier, the coalition of the 1960s broke down, at least one of its principles became institutionalized: diversity is positive and desirable. It is this principle that gives us a starting point for building a new consensus.

We are a nation that is more comfortable with its diversity of color, class, gender, and generation than we have been at any time in our history. Our diversity, and our comfort with it, are the basis for building the consensus we must structure. This starting point of affirming our diversity is a form of embracing the politics of inclusion and opportunity, the agenda of political religion, or Christian Populism.

By definition, in our diversity is a view broader and more illuminating than we possess individually. Some of us are old enough to remember the horror of the Holocaust and when racial discrimination was legal in the United States. But some are too young to remember apartheid American-style. Some of us remember when protest was the political art form of the day, we recall the heroic deaths of Schwerner, Cheney, and Goodman, and savor memories of the days when the Civil Rights and Voting Rights Acts were passed. But some are so young that they really can't understand all the furor or fear that surrounded the extension of the Voting Rights Act, because in their time there have always been voting rights.

Some fought and others watched on TV—in living color—the war in Vietnam. We came to know the futility and fatality of one country trying to impose its will on another. We came to know war for what it really is; it's not really heroic, but hell. But some are so young as not to have been made cynical by war and can remind us that there is something about America worth celebrating. This expansive view that is ours when we share our perspectives is our strength. Because of this we have an insight, but we also have an innocence. We have seen and know the best of what we can be. We also know that we are not yet what we can become.

The politics of consensus is driven by a "vision"; but the consensus is realized ultimately because of the players who are willing to come together to give form to that vision. In terms of consensus building, this means that the more expansive the vision, the more expanded must be the network of persons shaping the vision. If the vision is one of a community that is just and harmonious across color, class, gender, and generational lines, then the shaping of that vision must involve persons who cut across color, class, gender, and generational lines. The process of bringing people together to shape the vision causes them to "buy into" the vision, because they can see a picture that they can help to embellish by embracing it.

Again, this new consensus is about more than what we traditionally have called coalition politics. In traditional political coalitions, people come together because of a *mutuality of interest*, reflecting a "you scratch my back, I'll scratch yours" mentality. The politics of consensus reflects something more; it reflects *an interest in our mutuality*. It is not whether we ignore or accommodate special interests;

the fundamental issue is whether we take a national interest in those for whom we must have a special concern.

In the land of opportunity we cannot ignore the fact that for some persons, opportunities are few or nonexistent. We can and must build a new consensus that is forged on the premise that individual survival must be seen in the broader context of everyone's survival. We are inextricably bound to one another. As such, we must perfect the work that has brought us this far in our journey to togetherness. We must inspire a new spirit of hope and harmony, justice, and opportunity. We must work to continue to shape community consciousness, so that class, color, and custom are causes for celebration rather than contention. We have the foundation to fulfill this mission.

I believe that with the help of God—in whom there is "no Jew or Greek . . . slave or free . . . male and female"— and the leadership of the church, we can forge a new consensus, built on a paradigm that emphasizes unity with understanding, peace with parity, harmony with honorable intentions toward one another, and justice with gestures of human kindness and love. If the church is willing to be the lead witness, calling all flesh to see a common vision and live a common dream, we will be able to behold a new thing from Soweto to South Boston, from Lebanon to Liverpool, from Germany to Jerusalem, from Poland to Peking, from Rwanda to Russia.

THE CHURCH, PUBLIC POLICY, AND POLITICAL CAMPAIGNS

The problem that the liberal church has in becoming a prominent political player exists, in part, because of the theology that has informed much of its political action over the past few decades. Starting with James Cone's *Black Power and Black Theology* (1969), and his dictum "freedom by any means necessary," the character of much of the political theology of this period was established. Much of the political theology of this period (liberation, feminist, and Third World theologies) presupposed a revolutionary context as the environment for political action. The theology of this era had, implicitly or explicitly, a threefold aim: (1) to define political change as a revolutionary versus an evolutionary process, (2) to reinterpret salvation in existential terms more reflective of Marxist ideology rather than in eschatological terms more reflective of traditional Christian theology, and (3) to legitimate violence as a means of political expression in order to effect revolutionary change.

My intent here is not to critique the veracity of these points as valid theological assumptions; in fact, they are very helpful in understanding the struggles of Third World nations. (This is why the liberal mainline denominations have been particularly effective in their advocacy for Third World causes.) My point is simply to suggest this particular framework is not very helpful as a basis for influencing U.S. domestic policy. I am not suggesting that the church can afford to be "America-centric" in doing theology, nor am I suggesting that we should be insensitive to the often limited options available for political expression and political action in other countries. But I am saying that the church in America must speak to its political mandate in light of the history, constraints, and opportunities inherent in our political system.

Within our political system the church has several obligations and opportunities. In the 1960s, the glory years in terms of the church's political leadership, the fight was to win the right for a substantial number of Americans to participate in the political process. Now, the issue is how to participate in the process rightly.

As I mentioned in the previous chapter, the church ought to have a word to say about why it is important to participate in the political process. While there is nothing sacred about democracy as political systems go, it most closely embodies the Christian value of the sanctity of the individual. In political terms, this means we all count equally and have interests that ought to be equally protected. Out of this flows the injunction for participation in the democratic process. For if one is to embrace the notion that "we all count" in the abstract, we must implement it in the concrete, which requires political participation. That we count not only legitimates democracy as a political process, it is, at one and the same time, the principle that ought to inform law and policy and provide the measure for sizing up politicians.

Further, involvement of the church in policy formulation and electoral politics gives specificity to its political concerns. A policy debate or political campaign clarifies where you stand; you are either for or against a particular issue, or you are for or against a particular candidate. Given that the church is called to provide political leadership, it is inevitable that specific stands are taken on particular issues and for or against particular candidates. This is as it should be.

Finally, the obligation to be engaged in the political process rests on the fact that involvement in the process matters, as we have noted in chapter 2 in the discussion of Reconstruction. The contrast between the Reconstruction and post-Reconstruction periods shows the difference political participation makes in the quality of life for Black people. In our time, we have seen the same qualitative difference in the lives of African Americans and other disenfranchised groups after the passage of the Voting Rights Act of 1965. Participation in the political process makes a difference; the church has an obligation and an opportunity to get involved in order to give substance to its justice agenda.

Policy Formulation and Action

One of the concrete ways to participate in the political process is through policy formulation and action.

 A policy, or more precisely public policy, is a proposal that results in (or defines the objectives of) legislation, regulation, or programs at various levels of government. It is also a set of guidelines providing a framework for institutional or agency procedures. What I address in this section is a way the church can approach formulating or changing a particular public policy. (This particular model also has relevance for affecting private policy.)

A grid of this model for policy formulation and action follows. The interactive nature of the model is evident; that is, one can see how the factors at each level influence the other factors. In addition, the comprehensiveness of the effort to formulate and change public policy is clear. The grid shows how the process ought to hang together and indicates where gaps might appear in the pursuit of a particular policy objective.

A Model for Policy Formulation and Action

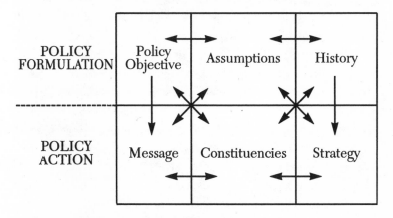

Perhaps the best way to explain the grid is to use as an example a policy issue in which I have been involved. In July 1993, President Clinton charged the nation's bank regulators with the task of revising the Community Reinvestment Act (CRA) so that the regulations would focus on performance rather than process. That is, the president felt that the fundamental principle guiding CRA should be that it result in equal access to credit, capital, and services for the minority community and other capital-starved communities. The effect of this reform was to be the inclusion into the economic mainstream of those historically mired in the economic swampland. A particular point of policy that was of concern to the network I head was the need for the new regulations to reflect a policy requiring banks to disclose, by race, the business loans they make. I will outline the process for policy formulation and action by offering examples of how we approached the policy change we sought regarding the disclosure of business lending data.

There are basically three factors that are relevant to the process of policy formulation. These are the policy objective, the assumptions one brings to the deliberations, and the history of matters relevant to the particular policy one hopes to advance. An explanation of each follows:

(1) The policy objective, in short, is the policy statement. It is the individual's, institution's, or political party's perspective of the political problem or issue that needs to be addressed. The policy objective reflects the problem, facts, and research relevant to formulating a response to the problem. In our effort to have an impact on the new CRA regulations, our policy objective was rather straightforward: we wanted the new regulations to require banks to publicly disclose and quantify by race their business lending patterns.

(2) The assumptions are the theological, ideological, or philosophical presuppositions with which one views the world. One's assumptions represent the basis for formulating the criteria that must be satisfied for the problem to be solved; i.e., how one views the world reflects one's views of how the world ought to be. One's assumptions also reflect how one identifies oneself in terms of color, class, community, gender, and generation. In summary, one's assumptions reflect one's sense of identity and loyalties and thus inform one's view of

the political problem and policy formulation. As an advocate for the interest of minorities, the assumptions I brought to the analysis of the regulations and the formulation of policy were distinctly racial. In addition to this perspective, one might have had one's thinking on this issue shaded by considerations of class or gender.

(3) The history is the record of what has happened before that is relevant to the formulation of a particular policy. The history includes relevant past and present policy, prior and present regulations, legislation, research, and positions of advocates and opponents regarding the particular issue. A primary question raised in this regard is whether this has been tried before and where the effort led. The relevant historical data for us on the issue of CRA regulatory reform included: no existing policy allowing for disclosure of business lending; a new policy of disclosure for mortgage lending with the result that once that policy took effect lenders moved to make their lending practices more fair; and the fact that Whites own thirty times the number of businesses than Blacks.

After the formulation of a policy, the next step is the enactment of that policy. The enactment of a particular policy (i.e., policy action) requires attention to several strategic concerns: how one crafts the message that summarizes the policy objective; identifies the relevant constituencies in the fight; and determines the appropriate strategy to get the policy objective enacted. Again, the explanations follow:

(1) The message refers to the crafting of the policy objective succinctly, clearly, and cogently in order to galvanize a constituency powerful enough to effect the sought-after change. In an age in which media represent a powerful tool in effecting public policy debates, the matter

105

of crafting the message is particularly important. The critical question is whether you can condense it to a thirty-second sound bite. The objective is to make the message memorable. Things to consider in fashioning the message are the potential headlines, what sort of spin the message might trigger in potential news stories, whether the message can be couched in a catchphrase for a poster, whether it represents an idea or ideal the people remember, and if it ignites the spark that fires people to action. In the effort to effect the CRA policy on the disclosure of business lending data, we felt a message that would put bankers and regulators on the defensive and crystallize our concerns was "CRA Reform: The Illusion of Inclusion."

(2) Constituencies are the advocates and opponents of the policy that is being advanced. In the vernacular, this is identifying "who is with us and who is against us." The identification of the varying constituencies can be broken down further into subgroups along the lines of race, region, income, occupation, professional affiliation, and so forth. The purpose of this sort of categorization is to aid in finding ways to appeal for support of one's particular proposal. The constituencies in our battle over the reform of the CRA were rather easy to identify. On our side were groups like the Greenlining Coalition, ACORN, the Center for Community Change, and the Clinton administration; our potential allies were minority and women's groups. The opposition to our position came principally from the federal regulatory agencies (Federal Reserve Board and FDIC) and bank trade associations. The OCC (a third federal regulator) appeared to be isolated by the other regulators, but in support of the reform. In order for us to carry the day on this issue, it would be critical for the regulatory opposition to be isolated and for us to convince

some key members of Congress of the merits of our position. In addition, it was necessary to broaden the constituency in favor of the reforms. This would bring the regulators around on our policy objective.

(3) The strategy is the plan and tactics one intends to use in order to get a particular policy enacted. At this point, the interactive nature of this model should be apparent. The three factors relevant to policy formulation and the two other factors relevant to policy action are critical to determining the strategy. Within the context of these factors a critical rule of thumb is "know your opposition well; don't use a shotgun to kill a mosquito." On the other hand, "don't take a toothpick to fight an eight hundred pound gorilla."

In attempting to get a particular policy enacted, some useful strategic tools include money, media, community organization and mobilization, voter registration and mobilization, petitions, lobbying, and negotiation. In the best case, you are able to be deliberative, to "plan your work and work your plan." There are times when the fight is brought to you because someone else has initiated the same process to effect change in a policy you support. When you are on the defensive, you should be as conscious as possible of the necessary factors to support your position. There are times when events move so swiftly that you bluff as a way to check the opposition and give yourself time to prepare. If that doesn't work, retreating becomes a viable option because it represents an opportunity to prepare for waging the battle at a more favorable time, under more favorable conditions. One example of the strategy we employed in order to make the case for our position was to testify before the U.S. House of Representatives Subcommittee on Consumer Credit and Insurance of the Committee on Banking Finance and Urban

107

Affairs, formerly chaired by Congressman Joseph P. Kennedy II. Our strategy worked. Disclosure of business lending to minority communities by regulated banks has become part of the CRA evaluation process.

In addition to the strategic considerations given to fashioning the message and the matter of identifying the opponents and proponents of your position, a critical question in mapping a strategy for policy action is the context of the debate. What is the political climate? This question is critical to determining whether you can win—or how much you can win, if you can't get everything you want.

Becoming adept at the skill of policy formulation and action is critical if the church is to play a pivotal role in fashioning new opportunities to include those on the margins in American society, and to ensure that those who are newly integrated into the mainstream flourish. In addition to cultivating the skills necessary to affect public policy, the church must become skillful in the art of electoral politics.

Electoral Politics

To state the obvious, one aim of an election is to elect people to public office. The aim of the church should be to elect people who give primacy to the justice agenda of the church. To reiterate a point made in chapter 3, who churchfolk support should be determined not by political party, but rather by the policies to which a political candidate is committed. (While I will discuss the church's participation in the electoral process in terms of how it relates to electing people to public office, it is important to note than the same principles for participation in the electoral process would apply to a referendum issue.)

Electing politicians who would be accountable to the justice agenda of the church requires: (1) articulating a political vision so people are clear about why they ought to support a particular candidate and so politicians will know the standard by which they are being measured; and (2) maximizing participation in the political process (i.e., voter registration and mobilization).

All too often the focus of discussion about a political campaign is simply on which person can win. Much of the conversation sounds as if the political equivalent of the Kentucky Derby is being discussed. The talk is about how this or that candidate might run in a crowded field, the more sophisticated use different indices (campaign organization, cash, constituency, record, and the candidate's vision) as they try to "handicap" the candidates. But the question is still the same: Which candidate will win the political prize?

While who wins is obviously important, on what basis the person wins is particularly important, especially for those at the apex of the church's concern about justice— minorities, women, and the poor. For many, if not most, White Americans, the quality of life relative to one another does not change drastically with the passing of the torch from one politician to the next. But for minorities, women, and the poor, strong political leadership can make a critical difference in whether we experience the fullness of American's promise as the land of opportunity.

During my lifetime, the Great Society legislation ushered through by President Lyndon Johnson is without a doubt the most profound affirmation of this point. Obviously, Johnson's efforts did not represent a panacea, but the results are as telling as they are dramatic: the numbers of African Americans graduating from college quadrupled; in 1960, 18 percent of Black families were middle class and by 1990 that number was up to 42 percent; and the percentage of Black elected officials has risen some 3000 percent!

Given the crucial difference that political leadership can make, the first issue that must be addressed in a political campaign is: What is the standard by which candidates will be judged as the basis for support? Given that the political, legal, and social foundation for opportunity has been laid, *the* issue for our time is extending opportunity to the economy. The facts confirm this mandate:

- At least forty million Americans live in poverty.
- Nearly half of all Black and Hispanic youth live in poverty.
- At least twelve million Americans are unemployed.
- Entry-level jobs in the manufacturing sector that pay $470 per week are being replaced by entry-level jobs in the service sector that pay $260 per week.
- The average White family in America is worth $43,000, and the average Black family is worth $4,300.

Based on these statistics it should be clear that the litmus test for leadership that anyone seeking public office must satisfy is: What would you do to make economic opportunity real for all Americans across color, class, gender, and generational lines? Because of the lack of economic opportunity for many minorities and women, it is critical that we know a candidate's capacity to understand and capability to address this problem. If a candidate is to demonstrate an understanding of the church's justice agenda, we must ask and demand a candidate's answers to three basic questions:

(1) Do you understand the extent of the lack of economic opportunity in America and how it affects the quality of life for those on the margins of this economy?

(2) How is your vision of a society in which economic opportunity is real for minorities, women, and the poor central to your primary policy agenda? (The point here is that all too often this issue is raised *after* everything else is addressed.)

(3) What *specific* policy and programmatic agenda would you advance to facilitate greater opportunity for minorities, women, and the poor in the mainstream of the American economy?

In addition to these general questions, there are some specific questions that must be answered. While not exhaustive, questions such as these are critical:

- What are the present and future opportunities for growth in the economy—nationally and locally?
- How can the public sector be a stimulus for economic growth and the inclusion of those historically marginalized in our economy?
- What options do we have to address structural unemployment in our country?
- How can small business development facilitate a more inclusive economy?
- What can be done to facilitate greater access to capital for minority and female-owned businesses, particularly those committed to locating in depressed urban areas?
- What employment and procurement models could be utilized to increase mainstreaming of minorities and women?

111

It is also important to note that while the focus of these questions is on minorities and women, these issues are relevant for the economy as a whole. That importance is reflected in a couple of ways. First, however we hyphenate our identification as Americans, we are all Americans. When any segment of the population is underutilized or excluded from the mainstream of the economy, the economy as a whole suffers. A chain is only as strong as its weakest link. Second, concern for minorities and others who are disadvantaged reflects the common good, because their problems could become the common plight. As a nation we are discovering something Joseph Lowery, President of the Southern Christian Leadership Conference, said some years ago: "When Black America has pneumonia, the rest of America has the sniffles." The African American community is often the bellwether of things to come. Problems such as disinvestment in the Black community and the undereducation of Black youth have given a structural character to the problem of poverty in the African American community. No solutions were sought. Now the same sort of structural problems are occurring in the country as a whole, and we have no model for action. In the face of national disinvestment, precipitated by a growing national debt and the loss of our competitive advantage in the world (due in part to the lack of investment in education generally), we are seeing the same structural problems in the nation that have existed for years in the Black community. We are now beginning to see the emergence of a White underclass! Again, the problem of minorities and women are not marginally important, but reflect the essence of what is wrong in the nation. This insight must be central to our political vision.

This sensibility must inform the standard by which we judge political candidates and our political leaders.

Beyond offering a clear perspective on what matters for us politically, the empowerment of the disadvantaged and disenfranchised is equally important. For them the point is as basic as the proverb: "Give someone a fish and he eats for a day; teach him to fish and he eats for a lifetime." One's political meal ticket is assured in three ways: voter stabilization, registration, and mobilization.

One problem that has surfaced in the attempt to develop a voter base among the disadvantaged in urban minority communities is that of election commissions routinely and indiscriminately dropping significant numbers of minorities from the voter rolls. The result of such tactics is an unstable political base.

In the effort to stabilize a constituency for the church's political agenda of justice and opportunity, what better voice is there for those who are disenfranchised than the church? What other body has the organization, independence, and moral authority to cause others to take notice of this concern to include the disenfranchised in the political process and to protect their right to be included? The Church can address this problem by monitoring election department activity and by holding officials accountable to their mandate to protect the franchise of minorities. This problem can also be addressed by continually mobilizing the community for participation in the electoral process.

The second key to political empowerment is voter registration. Once again, to use the African American community as an example, a primary impediment to the Black community's developing its political muscle is that only 50 percent of those eligible to vote are registered. And, on average, only 50 percent of those who are registered actually vote. Black people do not have the luxury of participating in the political process at 25 percent of their potential. I have found that a vigorous effort to register people based on the potential political power they possess results in their registering to vote. In other words, if you give people a reason to vote they will register.

Because the political values and virtues of the church are consistent with the fundamental tenets of democracy, it is logical that the church be in the vanguard of encouraging the disenfranchised to participate in the political process by registering to vote. In addition, the church is an ideal site for voter registration. It is viewed as a safe haven for those who might otherwise be intimidated because they have encountered indifference or even hostility to their participation in the political process. The church must invest in voter registration and advocate the need for universal registration until it is a reality. The church must see the political empowerment of the disenfranchised as a vital part of its mission.

Since the election of accountable officials is the bottom line of this process, a commitment to voter mobilization—getting out the vote to put people in office—is crucial. This is a relatively simple and straightforward matter. It requires supporting a particular candidate, crystallizing the importance of issues addressed in the campaign, developing a mechanism for getting people to the polls, and carrying out the plan. The church has the organization, the message, and the masses to provide this sort of leadership. The church has what it takes to provide leadership in the political arena.

CHAPTER SIX

JESSE JACKSON AND PAT ROBERTSON
Preachers and Politics

I n 1988, the candidacies of the Reverends Jesse Jackson
and Pat Robertson were the political equivalent of the
soap opera *As the World Turns*. None of the other
candidacies, on either side of the partisan strip, generated
as much interest and anxiety. No others had the same
potential as theirs to change the political landscape.

While the two shared the same profession, which made for
some similarities in their campaign styles, there were profound
differences in their campaigns' substance. To understand their
differences requires more than a superficial reading of their
most obvious differences of race and party affiliation.

The difference between these two pastors can be
summed up in their different religious testimonies and
political agendas. Their mixing of theology and politics is
such that in one we have a clear-cut conservative, whose
brand of conservatism results in the politics of pietism
reflective of the apostle Paul. In the other, we have a
progressive whose politics are populist in the tradition of
the prophets and the gospel.

An analysis of the candidacies of Jackson and Robertson shows why being religious does not necessarily result in identical political behavior, and shows why one religious perspective, over against the other, precipitates a political agenda more appropriate for our time.

The Campaigns: Structure and Strategy

Both the Jackson and the Robertson campaigns were, in many ways, a symbiosis between church and politics. The most obvious evidence was in the candidates themselves—preachers—running for president. Second, in terms of style and support, the mark of the church was most evident.

The rallies for the candidates took on the fervor of old-style church revivals. It was not unusual for a choir or two to be present. The call to register to vote had the familiar ring of a call to discipleship. Campaign contributions were raised by passing the plate as is common during Sunday morning church services.

More significant than style, the support of the church was equally evidenced in their campaigns. In an analysis of the Jackson campaign, Thomas Cavanagh and Lorin Foster noted: "The black church was an important element in the Jackson campaign. Black ministers frequently emerged as the chairmen of local Jackson organizations. Virtually everywhere, black ministers solicited both financial and organizational support."[1]

Meetings and rallies for the campaign were often held in Black churches, and rightly so. After all, where else but in the church would it have been appropriate for Black folks of Oxon Hill, Maryland, to gather to hear Jesse Jackson?

A story on the Jackson campaign in *Time* magazine captured the significance of the Black church to the Jackson campaign. In the seven predominantly Black denominations in this country there are seventeen million members in some sixty-one thousand congregations; in addition, there are Blacks in predominantly White Protestant denominations (The United Methodist Church, the United Church of Christ, the Presbyterian and Episcopal churches). It was to this huge potential political force that the campaign directed much of its attention. All the signs indicated that there was strong support for Jackson in the Black church.

The endorsement of key Black church leaders can certainly be interpreted as one clear sign of support. Jackson had the support of the Reverend J. O. Patterson, president of the Church of God in Christ, the United States' largest Pentecostal body, and the Reverend T. J. Jemison, president of the National Baptist Convention U.S.A. Jemison endorsed Jackson and was quoted as saying that between 90 percent and 95 percent of the denomination's ministers supported him. Beyond these two, the list of Black preachers endorsing Jackson was legion.

The importance of the endorsement of the Black clergy should not be underestimated, for as conventional wisdom has it, "as goes the Black preacher so goes the Black church." This support was forthcoming because the Jackson campaign represented the reconciliation and redemption offered by the Black church's participation in electoral politics. Jackson personified the creative tension with the other candidates and with the political establishment felt by Black people and articulated by Black preachers. As a result, the campaign generated a consciousness never achieved before in this country. Candidates were held

117

accountable on issues of racism, sexism, and economic justice as never before.

Pat Robertson's campaign was as vested in the evangelical and charismatic religious communities as Jesse Jackson's was in the Black church. Just as Jackson benefited from the endorsement of influential clergy, Robertson benefited from the endorsements of Oral Roberts and Jimmy Swaggart, until their "falls from grace" for fundraising and sexual improprieties. Robertson's campaign certainly would not have been perceived as viable, much less formidable, without the network of support he cultivated through his "700 Club" television program and his Christian Broadcasting Network.

In his book titled *Pat Robertson: A Personal, Religious, and Political Portrait*, David Harrell notes the importance of Robertson's church-based network to his candidacy:

> On September 17, 1986, Robertson had announced that he would run if three million registered voters signed petitions within the next year saying that they would work, pray, and give to support his race. . . .
> The logistical problems in the petition drive had been formidable, but his organization had done it. . . . Volunteers had counted and recorded the three million names. . . . The letters smacked of the common folk of the nation. Some were on the stationery of village churches. Most began with the words: "Dear Brother Pat."[2]

From Harrell's perspective, there was no doubt that when Pat Robertson formally became a candidate for the Republican Party nomination for president of the United States of America, evangelical and charismatic Christians got him to that point. The juice for Robertson's hoped-for juggernaut was supplied by his people.

Even the fears the evangelical church community had about Robertson's candidacy reflected their sense of its symbiosis with the evangelical church and the charismatic movement:

> Some expressed fears that Robertson's political ambition would damage CBN [Christian Broadcasting Network], the most respectable and formidable voice of charismatic Christianity. Others feared that Robertson would be "humiliated," and that evangelicalism would be damaged. Or, some evangelicals suggested, the candidacy of Robertson would separate the evangelical voting bloc into an outsider minority, killing its potential to influence the practical politics of the nation. And some of his close friends worried about the impact of his presidential ambitions on his ego and his spirituality. At the end of 1986, Jamie Buckingham, the coauthor of Robertson's autobiography, asked a series of questions: "Will Pat the Candidate no longer be our friend, our source of inspiration and accurate information, our analyzer of world affairs, our number one ministerial statesman?"[3]

Inside and outside the campaign, for positive results and negative implications, there was an acknowledgment that the candidacy of Pat Robertson was clearly rooted in the evangelical church and charismatic movement.

The Political Problematic

The personal, intellectual, and historic legacy each candidacy represented determined its sense of the political problematic of our time as well as its domestic and foreign policy agendas. Let me pause to define what I mean by the term *political problematic*. It is, substantively, what Ernst Troeltsch in *The Social Teachings of the Christian*

Churches calls "the social problem." According to Troeltsch the social problem includes the "new problems and duties we face in the ordering of social life in the modern social situation."[4] Troeltsch's definition is helpful in this effort to reconstruct the conceptual framework out of which Robertson and Jackson operate. I have chosen to call the matter to be resolved the political problematic rather than the social problem because while Troeltsch's definition implies a place for the mission agenda of the church and the political agenda of political campaigns, it does not clearly define the place of resolution for the major problems of society as the political arena. Another reason I have chosen to use the term political problematic is that this chapter is about two preachers running for political office. To talk about their focus as the resolution of *the political problematic* instead of *the social problem* is more precise.

In terms of their personal stories, Jackson and Robertson represent an absolute study in contrast. While both Jackson and Robertson are southerners by birth and are charismatic leaders, they have little else in common.

Jesse Jackson was born the son of an unwed teenage mother. The town in which he was born and lived was so incensed by his out-of-wedlock birth that his mother was kicked out of the church she had attended all of her life. Jackson grew up on the Black side of town in segregated Greenville, South Carolina. His intellectual and athletic abilities enabled him to attend the University of Illinois. Because of the racism he encountered in the classroom and on the athletic field, he transferred to the historically Black North Carolina Agricultural and Technical College.

During Jackson's college days the Civil Rights Movement was in full swing. As a student, he displayed the talent and temperament to be a leader in the politics of protest, and thus he was.

Pat Robertson was born in Lexington, Virginia. His mother's family tree includes Sir Winston Churchill; his father's family line goes back eleven generations to the first English settlement at Jamestown. It includes Benjamin Harrison, a signer of the Declaration of Independence, and two American presidents. Robertson's father, A. Willis Robertson, was a one-time senator from Virginia.

Robertson graduated Phi Beta Kappa from Washington and Lee University; from there he went on to Yale Law School.

If Jesse Jackson's life was one of protest, Pat Robertson's was one of privilege. Life viewed from the bottom up looks significantly different from life viewed from the top down. These respective vantage points are reflected in their views of the world. The origins of these two men bring an obvious logic to their respective political ideologies and religious orthodoxies. It becomes all the more clear why they understand the political problematic of our time as they do.

For Jesse Jackson, the political problematic is "racism" and "exploitation." His view is reflective of those of the nineteenth-century French scholar Alexis de Tocqueville and the twentieth-century Black scholar W. E. B. DuBois. In his four-volume classic, *Democracy in America*, de Tocqueville cited the "race problem" as the number one threat to American democracy. Some fifty years later DuBois echoed the same sentiment when he said that the preeminent American problem is the "color line." Some seventy years later Jesse Jackson gave this political problematic expression within the context of a presidential campaign.

Though Jackson sees race as key in understanding the political problematic of our time, it is critical to note that for him the matter of race is indicative of the political problematic and not definitive of it. He made this point in a speech at Northeastern University in 1984. He said: "Be clear; blacks alone are not the victims of [bad government policies]. We simply are the weather vane, signaling what is ahead for the rest of society."[5]

The issue of race represents a refinement of the contemporary political problem, which is exploitation. For Jackson the problems of color and class are simply different sides of the same coin.

The attention Jackson gives the exploitation of "the least of those in our midst" places him in the political tradition of populism. Given his religious orientation, he is a Christian Populist. This bent is evident in his domestic and foreign policy agendas.

In summarizing his domestic policy agenda to the 1988 Democratic National Convention in Atlanta, Jackson was quite precise in his analysis of the contemporary political problematic and how we solve it. We need, he said,

> a government that is the tool of democracy in service to the public health, education, affordable housing (of the masses), not an instrument of aristocracy in search of private wealth. . . . The moral challenge of our day is economic violence. Plants that close on workers without notice . . . consumers gouged by corporate greed. . . . a minimum wage that keeps workers in poverty.[6]

This same sense of the contemporary political problematic is also reflected in Jackson's foreign policy agenda. The essence of the political problem internationally is not the question of East-West hegemony; rather, it is the exploitation of the South by the North, the Third World by the First World, and the lesser developed countries by developed countries. As with his domestic policy agenda, Jackson clearly and concisely laid out his foreign policy concerns in the same speech. He said: "We must change our policy towards the Third World. Support international law. Respect self-determination. Defend human rights. Foster economic growth. Be consistent."[7]

In other words, our foreign policy and our domestic policy must respect the dictates of justice and equity and reflect the fundamental tenets of democracy, which are the hallmark of our republic.

During his run for the presidency, Jackson's policy agenda clearly reflected the politics of Christian Populism. That agenda was one that gave the appropriate priority to the "rejected stone" becoming the "cornerstone" of our political concern and public policy agenda. His politics demonstrated a theological commitment to the equal worth of the individual and the necessity of our being advocates for the "least of those" in our midst. The focus of Jackson's political agenda was not so much delegitimizing the interest of the White majority on a national scale or the affluent on an international scale. It was calling the country to embrace a vision emphasizing the neglected interests of minorities and women on the national level, and the less affluent South on the international level.

For Pat Robertson, the political problematic of our time is the "battle between secular humanism and the Judeo-Christian tradition" upon which this country was founded.[8] Translated in terms of his view of the world and his vision for it, this means, in terms of orthodoxy, Robertson is a Christian pietist. His understanding of the political problematic, in terms of ideology, translates into his being a political conservative.

The most revealing account of Robertson's politics and religion is found in his tome *America's Date with Destiny*. The book is divided into three parts. In part one, "Beginning Our Journey," he catalogues the great moments of American history that reflect America's fulfillment of its destiny. Those dates end in 1886. While the section includes a discussion of the evils of slavery and the benefit to the nation for having ended it, Robertson is equally pointed in underscoring President Lincoln's ambiguity on the issue of slavery and its secondary significance relative to the Civil War.

In section two, "Losing Our Way," he includes the founding of the American Civil Liberties Union, the election of Franklin Delano Roosevelt, and Lyndon Johnson's Great Society program.

Section three, "Finding Our Way Again," begins with the Spiritual March on Washington that took place in 1980 including the inauguration of Ronald Reagan as president in 1981. Nowhere in this section (or in the rest of the book) was there any mention of the Civil Rights Movement or Martin Luther King Jr. In a book on politics, through the eyes of a religionist, it is remarkable that there was no assessment of this period. He only alludes to the period with the negative assessment of President Johnson's Great Society programs, which were meant to institutionalize the initiatives the Movement embodied.

Robertson's personal story, and his understanding of history, says everything about his idea of how we resolve the contemporary political problematic. The solution, according to Robertson, "lies in less government, states' rights, and more individual integrity."

It is not that this view has no social agenda; it's just that there is no social justice component to that agenda! The diminished rank of social justice in Robertson's schema was evidenced most tellingly in his assessment of his father's defeat for reelection to the U.S. Senate. He was convinced his father's defeat was for the best because it removed him from Washington during Lyndon Johnson's Great Society, a period when the Democratic Party gave "itself over to pressure groups which advocate causes and initiatives which are contrary to the Bible and contrary to the Christian faith."[9]

This same assessment is echoed in political terms. In the chapter in which he discusses the impropriety and inadequacy of Johnson's Great Society programs, Robertson states that the "problems of poverty, inequality, and injustice are problems of the human spirit. And federal spending, even without limits, will never create a truly great society. The great society begins in the transformed hearts of the people, and it spreads one by one among us until the entire world is transformed."[10]

He makes an even more conclusive statement about the limitations of government in a discussion of poverty. He writes, "If a person is continuously in sickness, [or] poverty, . . . then he is missing the truths of the Kingdom."[11] Given this view, it is logical that his catalogue of social issues would reflect the conservative litany of the reasons for the moral collapse of America—the abuse of alcohol and drugs, and sexual promiscuity resulting in a veritable explosion of nudity, fornication, adultery, homosexuality, incest, child molestation, and sadomasochism.

David Harrell summarizes well how this understanding of the political problematic translates into an issues agenda for Robertson:

The "social issues" embraced three related but distinct areas of concern. . . . [First there are] the "family issues" [that] ranged from opposition to the Equal Rights Amendment to the pro-life crusade against unregulated abortion. The "moral issues" included such questions as drug abuse, pornography, and the regulation of television and motion pictures. Finally, the "education issues" included prayer in the public schools and demands for tuition tax credits for private schools.[12]

Robertson mixes politics and religion in a way that delivers a conservatism that results in political pietism. The focus in Robertson's schema is the individual versus the institutional, personal accountability versus public responsibility.

In Robertson's theology and politics we have crystallized the problems and pitfalls that are the crux of the issue I'm raising in this book. Religion and politics are mixed appropriately when the mix promotes the democratic ideal on which the country was founded, when it promotes the principle of the equal worth of every individual, which is the essence of the Christian ethical and political ideal. Jesse Jackson's brand of Christian Populism represents such a mix. Pat Robertson's approach would result in the obfuscation of the line between church and state. The goal of government in such a schema would cease to be the common good. Instead, the goal of government would be the imposition of a system requiring the conformity of individual beliefs and the abrogation of individual rights.

Assessing Jackson's Campaigns

The politics of Christian Populism, rather than the politics of pietism, is the way and role for the church in the political arena. While the Jackson campaigns weren't the perfect manifestation of Christian Populism, they were as close an approximation as we've observed on the national scene. Thus, what Jackson did is worth affirming and examining further.

While style and broad-based support are key indicators of the power of the confluence of religion and politics in the Jackson campaigns, the empowering alchemy of that matrix is even more profoundly expressed in the message and meaning of the campaigns.

From a purely political perspective the Jackson campaigns had four major objectives: (1) to increase Black participation; (2) to alter party rules and state laws to increase the electoral impact of this participation; (3) to articulate issues and positions of concern to minorities; and (4) to create a multiethnic coalition of progressive forces within the Democratic Party.

The first two objectives were designed to stimulate "creative tension" between the Black community and the political power structure by increasing the Black and progressive community's clout. The latter two objectives sought to reconcile disparate groups by articulating common issues and building coalitions. All four of the stated objectives served to disrupt established and institutionalized powers and consolidate access for marginalized groups.

While it is valuable and necessary to understand Jackson's candidacy in 1984 and 1988 as political phenomena, to view it solely from that perspective limits what one sees. Because the campaigns' style and support reflect the hand of the church, it is important also to interpret the substance of the campaigns in light of their roots and sustenance. The Jackson campaigns, more clearly than any in my memory, embodied the ecclesiological mission of redemption and reconciliation. These notes were consistently sounded from his campaign in '84 to the campaign in '88. In his announcement speech in '84 the themes were eloquently and passionately conjoined and represented the precursor of a more mature formulation of those themes in '88:

> This candidacy is not for Blacks only. This is a national campaign growing out of the Black experience and seen through the eyes of the Black perspective—which is the experience and perspective of the rejected. Because of this experience, I can empathize with the plight of Appalachia because I have known poverty. I know the pain of anti-Semitism because I have felt the humiliation of discrimination. I know firsthand the shame of bread lines and the horror of hopelessness and despair because my life has been dedicated to empowering the world's rejected to become respected. Thus, one perspective encompasses and includes more of the American people and their interest than do most other experiences.[13]

His announcement speech articulated an agenda of a new day and new way. The quantifiable and qualitative political objectives reflected in the Jackson campaigns need to be interpreted theologically to appreciate the full significance of what was accomplished. The real accomplishments of the campaigns were redemption and reconciliation.

Redemption

Quite literally redemption means to buy back freedom. In the context of the Judeo-Christian tradition it addresses the renewal of a right relationship with God. While redemption explicitly relates to the vertical relationship between God and humanity, it implicitly affects the horizontal relationship between people. This latter use of the word describes the reordering of political relationships within society. The underlying principle for this reordering is the quest to make society more just. To talk about this reordering of political relationships as redemptive implies a religious force and an edifying effect.

In a political sense, redemptive activity is an active rather than a passive process. It starts with a new definition of the self (individually and collectively) and a new definition of the political dynamic. Redefining one's self means understanding that "even in our fractured state, all of us count and fit somewhere"; or, more poetically, it means understanding that one's time has come. It's making the move (psychologically and emotionally) from "disgrace to amazing grace." Redefining the political dynamic means making a different assessment of political possibilities, discerning that

> leadership can mitigate the misery of our nation. Leadership can part the waters and lead our nation in the direction of the promised land. Leadership can lift the boats stuck at the bottom. . . . [It is understanding] our mission to feed the hungry, to clothe the naked, to house the homeless, to teach the illiterate, to provide jobs for the jobless, and choose the human race over the nuclear race.[14]

In an address after the 1984 campaign before a national Black sorority, Jackson outlined how the campaign had empowered his constituency. Though this was an assessment he offered after the 1984 campaign, the points he raised were equally applicable to '88. "What has the Jackson Campaign accomplished so far . . . ? We fought for and maintained our self-respect. We won some votes, and we lost some; we won some issues and we lost some; but fundamentally we won our self-respect. We raised the right issues. We interpreted the right issues. We fought for the right issues."[15]

Through Jackson's campaign Blacks were represented as policy makers as well as being represented at the polls in unprecedented numbers. Blacks have a permanently redefined role in the political process. The campaigns accomplished a series of empowering victories that cannot be overlooked. First, a whole new generation of political operatives gained experience. That would not have been possible were it not for the Jackson campaigns. A host of Black and progressive operatives were prepared to provide the input to make future campaigns more responsive to broader interests and constituencies.

A second empowering effect of the campaigns was the pride it generated among Blacks. Third, the fact that Geraldine Ferraro was the vice presidential nominee of the Democratic Party in 1984 and that Blacks, a Hispanic, and a Jewish woman were considered for the spot for the first time must be attributed to the Jackson candidacy. In the aftermath of the 1988 campaign, the Democratic Party elected a Black chairman—a reflection of the newfound status of Blacks in the party as a result of Jackson's run for the presidency.

A final effect of Jackson's campaigns was that some Whites crossed the "fear threshold" by seeing a Black person in the role of a presidential aspirant. Particularly for young people, the television image of a Black presidential candidate has had a profound impact nationwide. While this is difficult to gauge statistically, Whites can no longer dismiss the idea of a Black president, though they may see a Black candidate other than Jackson as the one.

The self-affirmation and redemptive advocacy reflected in these political achievements is renewing. It is perhaps the most profound affirmation of the ideals fundamental to democracy and Christianity—individual worth ("I count") and the need for the body politic to give priority to concern for the poor instead of the privileged. To cling to these claims and to give them currency is to practice the politics of redemption, the politics of Christian Populism.

Reconciliation

Aside from the redemptive mission of Jesse Jackson's campaigns, they were efforts committed to reconciliation. A commonsense understanding of reconciliation is that it restores unity beyond enmity. Some would argue that Jackson's campaigns were anything but unifying. They would point to the infamous "Hymietown" remark in '84 and the residual effect, which carried over to '88, as evidence. Without apologizing, it is important to place Jackson's controversial remarks in the '84 campaign (and the response it precipitated through '88) in their historical-cultural context if we are to understand the true intent of the campaign.

Historically and culturally, ours is a race-conscious society. Most of the time this has been expressed negatively. If we are at all honest we must admit we know the derogatory terms used to describe other ethnic groups, and we must confess that those words roll with much too great an ease from our lips. We've used the words as darts or felt their sting—kike, spick, mick, wop, nigger, honky. In such a context one's moral acumen should not be judged by whether one is possessed by demons that cause us to conceive and call people such things. Rather, the testament to our character is the extent to which we are willing to beat those demons back. From this angle, no more eloquent commitment to fighting the demon of racism has been stated than by Jesse Jackson at the 1984 Democratic National Convention:

> If, in my low moments, in word, deed, or attitude, through some error of temper, taste, or tone, I have caused anyone discomfort, created pain, or revived someone's fears, that was not my truest self. If there were occasions when my grape turned into a raisin and my joy bell lost its resonance, please forgive me. Charge it to my head and not to my heart. My head is so limited in its finitude, my heart is boundless in its love for the human family. I am not a perfect servant. I am a public servant, doing my best against the odds. As I grow, develop, and serve, be patient. God is not finished with me yet. . . .
>
> Even in our fractured state, all of us count and fit in somewhere. We have proven that we can survive without each other. But we have not proven that we can *win* or *make progress* without each other. We must come together.[16]

These were the words of a contrite heart and penitent spirit; this was the politics of reconciliation. As mentioned earlier, reconciliation is about restoring unity beyond enmity; as a process it is about forgiving transgressions and forging relationships. According to this understanding, the Jackson campaign was true to the process of reconciliation on both counts.

In terms of forgiving transgressions, a cornerstone of Jackson's commitment to reconciliation was his refusal to allow the Black experience to be embittering. Rather, he urged Blacks to view their experience as one that engendered empathy. He described forgiveness as being able to look beyond the pain to paradise, as moving from "finger-pointing to clasped hands, turning to each other rather than on each other." This is the stuff of reconciliation.

Reconciliation implies either healing a breach in an existing relationship or creating a relationship in the absence of one. Because Blacks and Whites were political equals during the period of Reconstruction, the issue of forgiveness as a precedent to reconciliation is a first-rank concern. But the question remains: If the Jackson campaigns were about reconciliation, to what extent were new relationships forged and old relationships healed?

The ultimate vindication of this goal would have come with Jackson's getting the nomination. The logic of the numbers supports this. White voters are the majority; to have gotten the nomination would have required at least a significant minority of White votes. This certainly would have signaled that a new community had come together. But, despite the fact that Jackson did not get the nomination in '84 or '88, meaningful relationships were forged during the process of those campaigns.

No other campaign could boast the visible diversity reflected in the Jackson campaign—a diversity present from the day of his first announcement. On the platform to endorse his candidacy were Latinos, Native Americans, nuclear freeze advocates, farmers, politicians, community activists, gays and straights, Blacks, Whites, and Asians. This was certainly a reflection of the bridges that had been built between many different communities.

No other campaign took the message to the ghettos, barrios, and Indian reservations of this nation. Jackson's workers reached out and reached back in ways unique to this campaign.

Statistically, there is evidence that the Jackson campaign made inroads into non-Black communities on election day. The Jackson campaign consistently attracted more non-Black votes than the others attracted non-White votes.

As the reconciling force, none would argue that the Jackson effort was the panacea, but the results were promising. The "rainbow" concept enabled some Americans to cross color and class lines and to claim a common political destiny.

The Jackson campaigns were in many ways an exemplary mix of religion and politics. The mix was by no means perfect; but the articulation of the mission of Christian Populism—redemption and reconciliation—was nearly perfect.

The campaigns were indeed a quest for power. But the quest did not obviate the passion for political, economic, and social parity for the least of those in America. Although power was a goal of the campaign, the campaign's mission remained wedded to mercy. The Jackson campaigns clearly established justice as the measure for the right mix of politics and religion.

PROPHECIES
Political Armageddon or Religious Renaissance?

A book like this, which deals with issues and actions in the past and present, would be incomplete without some projections for the future. In religious terms that is called "prophecy"! Prophecy is not mystery in a hocus-pocus sense; it is mystery in the sense that it speaks with certainty about that which is yet to be. Prophecy is the art of reading the signs of the times. Prophecy is the work of the church.

Given the present debate on the role of religion in the public square, a central prophetic question to be dealt with is "Will the religious right or left win the present battle in America's public square?" The answer to this final question is the bottom line of this chapter.

As I stated in the beginning of this book, the public— and politically sensitive—argument in which Americans are engaged about the role of religion in our political life essentially reflects a struggle for power. It is not simply an argument about whether religion ought to influence politics, though many couch the present controversy in those terms. The present controversy over religion and politics is really a fight about whose religion and whose politics will determine the national agenda. It is a battle between the political left and the political right, liberals and conservatives, new orthodoxies and old orthodoxies, progressive forces and oppressive forces.

The source of the present controversy is that the political right (including Christian Fundamentalists) has now launched a rearguard assault against the liberal political establishment to regain the political hegemony that was once theirs.

Let me not mince words. The rule-or-ruin political strategy of the religious right to regain political power must fail! The political armageddon they have initiated threatens the very religious renaissance they purport to seek. People for the American Way,[1] which tracks the political activity of the religious right, found that they have initiated grassroots activity in every region in the country. Texas and California are two of their biggest battlegrounds, along with Georgia, Ohio, and Virginia. They are moving into less conservative states like Massachusetts, New York, and Minnesota, and they are making gains. Their targets of opportunity run the gamut from congressional seats to governorships to school board seats. The issues around which their quest for power centers include school prayer, abortion, and gay and lesbian rights. Their strategy is to take no prisoners, spare no quarter, and no distortion or half-truth is beyond use in order to further their cause. In the quest for political power they have perverted the biblical injunction to be as "wise as serpents and as gentle as doves" and have become wolves in sheep's clothing.

This strategy of deception has become most evident in their efforts to enlist the minority community in their cause. The religious right has on occasion co-opted the

PROPHECIES

Civil Rights Movement's leading hero—Dr. Martin Luther King Jr.—and co-opted the rhetoric of the Civil Rights Era in support of causes totally unrelated to civil rights, or in some cases, directly at odds with civil rights. People for the American Way, in a report documenting these efforts, notes:

> This new outreach effort is ironic given that over the years, these same right wing organizations have opposed virtually every initiative regarding civil rights. From their anti-integration activities of the '50's and '60's to their anti-affirmative action appeals of the '70's and '80's, from their support for Bob Jones University to their opposition to sanctions against South Africa, the Right has promoted a narrow, often divisive agenda that is inevitably at odds with the notion of equal justice. Today, in a cynical attempt to advance their political agenda, the Religious Right is turning to the minority community for organizing help.
>
> This new approach is best personified by the man who breathed life into the Religious Right, Jerry Falwell. In the '60's, as a minister in Lynchburg, VA, Jerry Falwell preached against integration. In the '80's, as leader of the Moral Majority, he advertised Kruggerands at the height of divestiture and called Bishop Tutu a "phony." And yet in the '90's, Falwell has sought to rally African-American support for his cause. In late 1993, for example, Falwell travelled to Philadelphia to visit Deliverance Evangelistic Church, an influential African-American church, to argue that African Americans should support his "pro-family" agenda. He has also begun to direct his anti-gay appeals to African-Americans, saying a person is a moral pervert by choice and should not be rewarded for being a minority ("Religious Right's Efforts at Outreach to Ethnic and Minority Communities," p. 1).

My objection to the agenda of the political right has nothing to do with their injection of religion into this

137

political discussion. The church has always been politically concerned. The biblical church was politically concerned. However you interpret Jesus' argument that you ought to give Caesar his due, or John's allegorical description in Revelation of his citizenship experience being like living in the belly of the beast, these are political concerns. In our time, Martin Luther King Jr. was politically concerned. To frame this matter of the church's political concern in the context of the present controversy, the attacks by Christians on American political leaders are not even new. When the nation's founding fathers excluded all mention of God from the Constitution in 1787, they were widely denounced as immoral and the document was deemed godless. Today's charges of America as godless have old and deep roots.

While the Constitution is supposed to be God-neutral and there should not be a religious test for eligibility for political office, there *is* a place for the role of morals in the common life of the country. This is a point on which most Americans would agree. In a poll by the *Wall Street Journal*, released in May 1994, respondents were asked their opinion about whether values should be taught in public schools. More than 90 percent felt that virtues like honesty, the Golden Rule, and even the acceptance of people of different races and religious persuasions would be appropriate subject matter. It was the sense of those polled that those values are important to the development of individual character and to the maintenance of the character of our country. Obviously, the church ought to have something to say in this regard.

Beyond addressing the issue of the role of morals and values in our common life, there are clearly moral dimensions to patently political issues. Certainly the church ought to have something to say and do in those matters.

Beyond the Civil Rights Movement there have been a number of contemporary cases in which people acting from a religious perspective have been deeply involved in shaping political events. In this vein, there was the Lutheran Church's involvement in the collapse of East Germany in 1989, and the involvement of Catholic and Protestant churches in South Korea's ultimate turn toward democracy in the mid-1980s. Again, my point is not whether the church ought to be involved in politics; the issue is the nature of that involvement. In the contemporary debate on the proper mix of religion and politics, the religious right is wrong! What I intend to do in the rest of this chapter is to explore several hot-button issues raised by the religious right and offer my thoughts on what the church's approach ought to be, address why the religious right must be defeated, suggest how they can be defeated, and offer my sense of what will happen relative to the religious right's present efforts.

The Issues

There are several hot buttons the religious right has pushed in order to try to galvanize a constituency in America. Those issues are prayer in school, abortion, and gay and lesbian rights. (One of the other issues that is part of the religious right assault is affirmative action. The arguments for why it is important were addressed in chapter 3.) Aside from the policy and life choice implications of each of these issues singularly, it is important to appreciate that cumulatively these issues represent an agenda that would disempower all those groups—Blacks, women, and gays and lesbians—who benefited directly and indirectly from the Civil Rights Movement of the '60s. It is also important to note that the religious right's approach is to raise these issues in such a way that they become wedge issues among those who ought to be allies in opposition to the agenda of the right.

Prayer in the Schools

While the issue of prayer in the schools has been clearly associated with the religious right, it is one of those issues on which many have an opinion; and those opinions are not as simple and clear-cut as saying we either ought to have prayer in the schools or we shouldn't have prayer in the schools.

As a matter of fact, according to Arthur Kropp, president of People for the American Way, polls indicate that 60 to 70 percent of Americans believe that some form of prayer in schools is appropriate. Opinions on this subject run the gamut from the tongue-in-cheek response that as long as we have math tests there will be prayer in schools, to the sentiment that in days gone by when everybody prayed in school things seemed much more under control. It is this later chord that has resonated in the African American community, where folks lament the almost battlefield conditions that define school life for so many youngsters.

Recently in Georgia, the state legislature passed a law mandating "a brief period of quiet reflection for not more than sixty seconds" at the opening of the school day. The driving force behind that law was not the religious right but a Black state senator, David Scott. The *New York Times* quoted Scott as saying, "After every shooting, after every kid is killed, what do they do? They get to their school, and they have a quiet moment of reflection. Now surely if it is good to do that after the killing, surely to incorporate a silent moment of reflection at the beginning of the day would go a long way in calming down, toning down, setting a mood." The logic of his position is striking.

For the vast majority of Americans who feel that some sort of prayer in schools is appropriate, the concern is not the political hegemony of the religious right. They are concerned about the need for our young people to have a more anchored moral life. They are concerned about the need for more civility in our common life. They are concerned about the carnage on our streets and how we stop it. Certainly it is hard to find these goals objectionable. If these are the goals of prayer in schools (and nothing else seems to be working), then what is the problem with prayer in school?

The problem is really rooted in the fact that as a nation we have a history of people and groups using religion as a club, thus adding to the incivility, disrespect, and intolerance that seem to be symptomatic of our time. It is hard to forget that the Reverend Bailey Smith, former president of the Southern Baptist Convention, proclaimed that God doesn't hear the prayers of Jews. Our schools are less homogeneous now than they were before *Brown v. Board of Education of Topeka* (1954). It is very possible that one of Bailey Smith's disciples is teaching in the classroom or is in the next seat. I would have a problem with either one of them leading my child in prayer.

While this fear is legitimate, I believe we can be faithful to our concern about the abuse of prayer and not be prevented from coming up with creative responses to our concerns about our fractured common life. I also believe

141

that concern does not have to result in a wholesale prohibition of prayer in the school or other public settings. We do have some options.

First of all, a moment of silence at the start of the school day is a legitimate alternative to calling for prayer to start the day. Such a moment of silence does not have to be posed as a mandate for prayer; it can and should be viewed as means to encourage young people to stop and get focused for the day. Suggesting that a moment of silent reflection represents a potential constitutional crisis shows the absurdity of how far the separation of church and state arguments are starting to go.

In addition to this option, for those who feel the day ought to start with prayer, churches or synagogues near schools could be encouraged to open before school to give those inclined to pray before the school day starts a place to do so.

In Atlanta one church has done just that. The Jackson Memorial Baptist Church, across the street from Harper High School, opens its doors before school to provide an opportunity for students and faculty to pray before the school day begins. That someone chooses to exercise this option is purely voluntary, and it clearly keeps intact the fire wall between church and state.

Another option that would enable us to address the concern about the lack of civility reflected in our schools and society is to teach character education in our schools. Not only would such a curriculum help with discipline problems in the schools, it is also an appropriate way to prepare young people for citizenship.

A May 10, 1994, article in the *Wall Street Journal* made a couple of interesting points. First of all, in settings where character education is taught, the number of school expulsions and fights dropped significantly. In addition, it is possible to structure a curriculum that focuses on such basic values as honesty, the Golden Rule, compassion, and discretion, and do it in a way that no one's moral sensibilities are offended. In developing such a curriculum, the Pattonville School District in St. Louis County, Missouri, decided that if anyone disagreed with a character trait, it would be discarded. They reached a consensus on twenty traits.

A final option in dealing with this issue of school prayer is to establish some ground rules for it. In addition to appealing for divine guidance and protection, offering prayers reflecting varying traditions is a tangible way of coming to appreciate other traditions and other people. Some of those ground rules for public prayer might be that prayers be inclusive, tolerant, affirming of our common life, and apolitical. When praying is a part of the routine there should be a rotation of religious traditions represented.

It is my sense that all of the alternatives I have laid out optimize the basic principle of justice and fairness that is at the root of Christian Populism. These alternatives are legitimate ways to move us beyond the religious right's inclination to use prayer as a political symbol and as the sanctification of their divisive political agenda.

Abortion

The religious right has framed the abortion issue the way the media and Americans seem to like their politics: You are either for or against an issue, you are either with us or against us. This issue is not that simple. Nor can all the relevant layers of consideration be reduced to the issue of choice. Though let me say unequivocally that should the religious right's position become policy, the primary victims will be women and their right and responsibility to exercise moral judgment on a matter that intimately involves them.

Within the context of the present debate about religion and politics, the range of moral and policy issues relevant to the abortion question is broad. First, the outcome, implications, and nuances of the abortion debate do not rest on the question of when life begins. Most Americans overwhelmingly support a woman's right to choose; that opinion is based on the accurate and commonsense assessment of the present policy that only abortions after the first trimester represent a moral and legal gray area. Ironically, it is the religious right's insistence on framing the debate in terms of the question of when life begins that they expose a fundamental contradiction in their position.

If their basic agenda in the abortion controversy is the affirmation of life, then their moral seriousness is eroded because there are some questions that they have failed to answer. For example, given their compassion for the unborn, how do they account for their callousness toward the now-born as reflected in antiwelfare and antijustice positions that would result in a life of misery of many of these children who would be carried to term? If the antiabortion movement is an affirmation of life, why is its response so muted regarding the murder of physicians at clinics where abortions are performed? Why don't we see the antiabortion movement putting its strength to work behind the efforts of groups like the Children's Defense Fund, which is committed to "leaving no child behind"? Why isn't the antiabortion movement more involved in trying to effect adoption and foster care policies and programs that are all-encompassing and more compassionate? How do they explain the moral contradiction of being both antiabortion and against sex education when studies indicate that sex education reduces pregnancy and promiscuity among teenagers?

And finally, how can the religious right presume an air of moral seriousness when in the name of life they would, by their abortion policy, deny women the essence of life choices? Is not the essence of a moral decision reflected in the decision to procreate or not? Should not a woman have the right to determine whether she would live a life of poverty or self-sufficiency, which is often at stake when poor women deal with the issue of pregnancy? Are these the sorts of decisions we would want our government to make? Is it not the individual's right and responsibility to make these sorts of moral decisions, and that these rights should be something that the government ought to be duty bound to protect? In a nutshell, fundamental to the issue of abortion is the interest and rights of women as moral agents. The basic question is: Doesn't justice require that a woman have rights that must be affirmed and respected?

Having laid out some critical questions, let me suggest some answers that reflect a Christian Populist perspective. First of all, the religious right's stance that abortions are wrong is a legitimate response to the question of whether a woman should have an abortion. However, it must be added that it is not the only response. It is one choice, and for other reasons there are other choices and other very legitimate considerations. These are implied in the questions raised earlier.

For women who agonize over the decision of carrying a pregnancy to term because of the labyrinth of impediments that make adoption a nightmare, we need to fashion policies that remove the barriers. For women who are on the economic margins in America, for whom a baby would result in poverty, we need to fashion welfare policies that enable them to move into the mainstream with educational opportunities that equip them for the future. Equal employment opportunity is an issue that must also be addressed if women are to be free in making such decisions.

For a woman who simply seeks to act as a free moral agent in making a decision about whether to carry a pregnancy to term, the government needs to ensure that she has the right to make such a decision without fear of criminal prosecution or recrimination. In other words, the role of government—if it is to respect the notion of the separation of church and state—should be to allow a woman to make such a decision as a matter of conscience between her and her God without the imposition of government. I believe these sorts of approaches represent the best mix of politics and religion and respect the integrity and role of each.

Gay and Lesbian Rights

The third pinnacle of the religious right's platform is its antigay and lesbian initiatives. The assertions that "AIDS is a judgment against America for allowing homosexuality to run rampant" and that "homosexuality is antisocial and pathological" serve as the pretext for legislative initiatives such as banning homosexuals in health care, day care, and teaching jobs; capping the spending on AIDS research and treatment; and requiring the reporting of AIDS "carriers."

Despite attempts to frame the debate on gay and lesbian rights as an issue of lifestyle, sexual preference, and piety, gay and lesbian rights is a civil rights issue. It is an issue of whether this society will continue to condone discrimination (or persecution) of an individual because of who he or she is. The point of intersection between our moral and constitutional traditions that is relevant to the issue of gay and lesbian rights is that all persons in this society, by virtue of their citizenship, have rights that have to be protected. In the language of the Bible the issue is that you "do unto others as you would have them do unto you," because *the value of our personhood is of equal weight*. From this perspective, just as there is no moral or legal justification for employment discrimination, or for violating the sanctity of anyone's home with injunctions that impinge on his or her lifestyle, or for denying them access to health care or the benefits of medical science because of who they are, there is likewise no justification for discriminating against homosexuals. The church ought to be saying this unequivocally and uncategorically.

The Prophecy

My prophecy about the outcome of the religious right's present power play is that it will fail. The 1994 elections saw Republicans take control of both Houses of Congress and a majority of the nation's governorships. While they could not have done so without the help of the religious right, I believe the religious right's effort to remake America in their image will ultimately fail.

The religious right must fail because the movement violates the fundamental principle of political participation by the church; that is, that the proper mix of politics and religion should be directed toward the "perfection" of democracy. By this I mean that justice, harmony, and opportunity must be the primary values informing our policies and politics. In the best sense of our constitutional tradition it means that "the minority is protected from the tyranny of the majority." In the best sense of our biblical tradition, it means giving special consideration to the "least of those in our midst." When looking at the political solutions of the religious right for fixing what is wrong with America, not many of these solutions are aimed toward these values. For example, their opposition to the Civil Rights Restoration Act because "churches would be forced to hire a practicing active homosexual drug addict as a youth pastor" and it would aid the agenda of radical feminists who are nothing but "frustrated lesbian man-haters who declared war on the male gender" does not seem to pass the justice test or harmony test for the appropriate mix of politics and religion. When leaders like the Reverend Jerry Falwell contend that "if a person is not a Christian, he is inherently a failure," he is not offering a pretext to promote policies that would guarantee equal opportunity. The religious right's quest for political hegemony must fail because it, first and foremost, fails the fundamental principle that ought to guide the church in politics.

Second, the religious right must fail because its practices and policies contribute to the increasing incivility that is beginning to define our body politic. Their abhorrence of dissent causes them to spare nothing in describing those they see as political enemies. The Reverend Jerry Falwell's contention that by acquiescing to "libertarians, the New Agers, the abortionists, the feminists, the radical homosexuals . . . we are allowing a little minority, three, four, five percent of radicals in this country in all those areas to literally rewrite American history and totally obscure the fact that America is a Christian nation" is indicative of the vindictiveness that erodes our common life and makes rational political discourse difficult if not impossible. Pat Robertson has said, "What Planned Parenthood is doing is absolutely contrary to everything Christian. It is teaching kids to fornicate, teaching people to have adultery, teaching people to get involved in every kind of bestiality, homosexuality, lesbianism—everything that the Bible condemns. And teaching to be without absolutely any moral restraint." This is certainly not the sort of stuff that enables discussion among organizations and individuals that espouse opposing views.

If the religious right is to be prevented from setting the political metronome to which the nation will march, there are a number of things that must be done.

First, the church must find its "political voice." The church must speak up in the face of the religious right's assault on justice, harmony, and opportunity in this country. The battle must be joined. The broader church has been curiously silent in the face of the religious right's assaults, or at best, disjunct in its response. Not only does the church need to better coordinate a response to the religious right, the church must assume the vanguard position in articulating the vision of healing and hope this nation so desperately needs. While the religious right has struck a responsive chord relative to the issue of moral decline in America, its narrowly defined moral agenda puts it at the margin of mainstream thought. The issue of moral myopia is a point on which the religious right is vulnerable. To expose that vulnerability the religious right must be countered on every point, challenged at every turn, and battled in every forum.

Second, if the agenda of the religious right is going to be defeated, the church must forge a new consensus. This does not mean finding a common denominator that will appeal to the basest urges of the broadest number of people; it means finding a common denominator that appeals to legitimate interests of the broadest number of people.

Technically speaking, America is a country of minorities—Hispanics, Blacks, gays and lesbians, Asians, to name a few. A lot of those minorities have a stake in seeing this justice issue take root. In addition, many other people fall into the class of the disadvantaged. Finally, there are those who know, or who have known, the sting of racism and should be able to benefit from a Christian Populist agenda. (After all, anti-Semitism is still a problem for Jews; and within our common memory there were signs in places like Boston that read "no dogs or Irish allowed.") When these groups are added together, a fairly broad cross section of people results, representing a significant political force. In order for this coalition to materialize, the call has to be issued for these groups to come together. For that call to be heard and heeded, the basis for that coming together must be clearly and cogently articulated. The church should do this!

If these varying groups are to come together, they must move beyond their hang-ups about "whose ox has been gored the deepest." Everyone's story of suffering, denial, and discrimination is as legitimate as the next; this is the common denominator. It is cause for coming together.

Finally, if the religious right is to be defeated, the vote must be mobilized on election day. In terms of political participation, this is where the rubber meets the road. In a democracy, it is the ability to get the vote out that determines whose politics and policies will carry the day. More specific to defeating the religious right's agenda are studies that indicate that when the turnout is highest, right-wing candidates do the poorest. Arthur Kropp, president of People for the American Way, examined the results of the 1994 school board elections in Westchester and Virginia Beach and concluded that "the lessons of these two elections is clear: when communities become fully involved in school board elections, right-wing backed candidates lose ground."

Although I believe the religious right's play for power will fail and that its failure might be ensured, let me add that its failure is not a fait accompli. There are a number of disturbing trends that suggest that the movement can find fertile soil. Two of those trends were reflected in a national survey by Peter D. Hart Research Associates. The first is that among noncollege educated voters a political candidate who emphasizes the value of diversity is more likely to be looked upon less favorably than one who does not. The second finding was that younger Americans (eighteen- to twenty-nine-year-olds) "feel significantly less negative toward the religious right than do voters in all other age groups." A third trend was reflected in a poll commissioned by the *Times Mirror* Center for the People and the Press and reported in the *New York Times* (9/21/94). It noted that 51 percent of White Americans now believe that equal rights have been pushed too far; this despite the fact that many of those same respondents feel that there has not been much real improvement in the position of Blacks in the United States. On the one hand, the trends are disturbing; on the other hand, they simply point to the fact that the church has work to do, and these trends clarify what that work must be.

Earlier I made reference to the year 1996 as a significant watershed in America relative to the issues of race, gender, and justice. That year will mark the hundredth anniversary of the *Plessy v. Ferguson* Supreme Court decision, marking the end of Reconstruction and America's first real experiment with democracy in the truest sense. During Reconstruction, Blacks received the vote and soon thereafter women received the franchise as well. Educational opportunity became a reality. America became a much more open and tolerant society. All of that ended with *Plessy v. Ferguson*. The nation returned to an era when Blacks had "no rights Whites were bound to respect." Soon other groups that had been empowered during Reconstruction were put "back in their place." If the religious right carries the day, some four decades of struggle will have been for naught. It would be a supreme irony that as South Africa is moving away from apartheid, America could well be moving toward apartheid—one country separate and unequal. Obviously, this nation has a choice as to which road it will take. What sort of signpost for the future will the church hold up?

THE CHURCH'S OBLIGATION

Why ought the church to be involved in the political process? It is an opportunity to do the right thing. Theologically speaking, the church has as its chief concern the disadvantaged and disenfranchised. Participation in the political process enables the church to move from the point of advocacy to efficacy. It enables the church to move from preaching to praxis in addressing needs.

For the Black church, in particular, involvement in the political process is an obligation. Bishop John Hurst Adams of the African Methodist Episcopal Church summarized the substance of that obligation in an address at the Fourth National Policy Institute of the Joint Center for Political Studies:

> The reading of the history of black America makes it quite clear that black people have made the black church the strongest and biggest thing black folks have got. Despite the growing diversity in our communities, and despite the erosion of the church's authority in recent years, the black church remains our strongest and biggest institution. It has the people, it has the organization, it has the history, and increasingly it has the leadership. Since black people have poured themselves and their resources into making

153

the black church our largest institution, it clearly suggests to me that the black church has an enormous obligation to black people.[1]

This observation has implications relative to the church's political involvement. Clearly if the political arena is one place where significant change can be realized for Blacks, then the church has an obligation to be there.

The church has been and is uniquely fit for action in the political arena. With the entrance of the religious right into politics in recent years, political pundits have discovered something that Black preachers, the Black church, and politicians have appreciated for years; that is, as voluntary associations go, the church is ideal for organizing and effecting the political process. Black preachers are quick to boast, and rightly so, that on Sunday morning they see more people more regularly than any other individual or organization owned and controlled by Black people. And a common belief system makes congregants potentially the most potent political force in the community. Despite the fact that the news media focused on this power only during the Jackson presidential campaigns, some Black churches have been registering voters, distributing literature, campaigning, and getting out the vote on election day for years. It has been commonplace in the Black community for politicians to address congregations during prime time in political seasons. All these activities represent the traditional involvement of the Black church in the electoral process.

The Black church has demonstrated that the church is particularly suited to be a player in the political game because it is independent. The church is one of the few institutions that the people—in a communal sense—own and control. Thus, the institution and individuals ministering within it are accountable first to God and second, to those folk who come and support the church. Thus the church can enter the portals of power unbeholden to anyone, and as such can be as bold and prophetic as the occasion demands, not mincing words or judgments. To become involved in the hurly-burly world of politics does pose a very stark choice for the church. Is the church going to be a sacerdotal functionary presiding over the misery of God's people on the margin of society? Or will it answer the prophetic call that requires it to challenge principalities and powers in the name of hope and justice? If the church is to be true to the tenets of its faith and the traditions of our culture, the choice is easy. It must enter the fray!

I must admit that there are risks in the church's involvement in the political process. Political activity can be a source of schism in the pews. There is the risk of misrepresenting the church's theology to the faithful. And pastors and parishioners can be prostituted in the process. But the call to live our faith is so compelling, and the context for action so clear that we must be prepared to "lose our [institutional] lives" in order to offer an authentic witness to the world.

N O T E S

Introduction

1. Robert McAfee Brown, *Spirituality and Liberation: Overcoming the Great Fallacy* (Louisville: Westminster, 1988), p. 33.

1. Politics and Religion

1. Ernst Troeltsch, *The Social Teaching of the Christian Churches* (New York: Harper & Brothers, 1960), p. 19.
2. Dorothee Soelle, *Political Religion* (Philadelphia: Fortress Press, 1974), p. 59.
3. Ernst Troeltsch, "Political Ethics and Christianity," *Religion in History,* trans. James L. Adams and Walter E. Bense (Minneapolis: Augsburg Fortress, 1991), p. 197.
4. Michael Harrington, *The Politics of God's Funeral: The Spiritual Crisis of Modern Civilization* (New York: Holt, Rinehart & Winston, 1983), pp. 7-8.
5. Troeltsch, "Political Ethics and Christianity," pp. 183-84.
6. Ibid., p. 184.
7. Jürgen Moltmann, *On Human Dignity* (Philadelphia: Fortress Press, 1984), p. 30.
8. José M. Bonino, *Toward a Christian Political Ethic* (Philadelphia: Fortress Press, 1983), p. 82.
9. Ibid., p. 83.
10. David Tracy, "In the Words of David Tracy," *The New York Times Sunday Magazine,* 9 November 1986, p. 28.
11. Cornel West, *Prophesy Deliverance! An Afro-American Revolutionary Christianity* (Louisville: Westminster Press, 1982), pp. 101-4.
12. John Hurst Adams, Joint Center for Political Studies, "Conference Report of the Fourth National Policy Institute," Vol. 12, No. 4, (April 1984), p. 6.
13. Cain Felder, *Troubling Biblical Waters: Race, Class, and Family* (Maryknoll, N.Y.: Orbis Books, 1989). See chapter 5, particularly

the section titled "Historical Roles on Preaching in the Black Church."

14. Paul Tillich, *Systematic Theology,* Vol. III (Chicago: The University of Chicago Press, 1976), pp. 369-72.
15. F. W. Beare, *The Gospel According to Matthew: Translation, Commentary, and Notes* (New York: Harper & Row, 1981), p. 492.
16. Cornel West, *Prophetic Fragments* (Grand Rapids: Eerdmans, 1984), p. 31.

2. The Civil Rights Movement:
A New Epoch in Church History

1. Lerone Bennett, Jr., *Before the Mayflower: A History of the Negro in America, 1619–1964* © 1962 Johnson Publishing Company, Inc., pp. 183-85.
2. Ibid., pp. 197-98.
3. Ibid., pp. 221, 235-36.
4. Cornel West, *Prophetic Fragments* (Grand Rapids: Eerdmans, 1984), p. 4.
5. Ibid., p. 5.
6. "Lowery Marks 40 Years Serving World Parish," *The Atlanta Journal/Constitution,* Section G, 22 October 1988.
7. James Washington, ed., *A Testament of Hope: The Essential Writings of Martin Luther King, Jr.* (New York: Harper & Row, 1986), p. xx.
8. Major J. Jones, *Christian Ethics for Black Theology* (Nashville: Abingdon Press, 1974), pp. 189-90.
9. James Cone, *A Black Theology of Liberation* (Philadelphia: J. B. Lippincott Co., 1970), p. 77.
10. Ibid., p. 79.

3. The Political Church in the Post-Martin Era

1. James Washington, *A Testament of Hope: The Essential Writings of Martin Luther King, Jr.* (New York: Harper & Row, 1986), p. 219.
2. Major J. Jones, *Black Awareness: A Theology of Hope* (Nashville: Abingdon Press, 1971), pp. 59, 60.

3. Stephen L. Carter, *The Confirmation Mess* (New York: Harper-Collins, 1984), p. ix.
4. The National Council of Christians and Jews, "Taking America's Pulse," 1994.

4. Forging a New Political Consensus

1. B. Kantrowitz, "A Tenuous Bond from 9 to 5," *Newsweek*, 7 March 1988, pp. 24-25.
2. Jesse Jackson's Keynote Speech to the Democratic National Convention in 1988, July 19, 1988.
3. Samuel D. Proctor and William D. Watley, *Sermons from the Black Pulpit* (Valley Forge, Pa.: Judson Press, 1987), p. 20.
4. *The United Methodist Hymnal* (Nashville: The United Methodist Publishing House, 1989). "In Christ There Is No East or West," no. 548.

6. Jesse Jackson and Pat Robertson: Preachers and Politics

1. Thomas E. Cavanagh and Lorn S. Foster, *Jesse Jackson's Campaign: The Primaries and Caucuses* (Washington, D.C.: The Joint Center for Political Studies, 1984), p. 13.
2. David Harrell, *Pat Robertson: A Personal, Religious, and Political Portrait* (New York: Harper & Row, 1987), pp. 4-6.
3. Ibid., p. 227.
4. Ernst Troeltsch, *The Social Teachings of the Christian Churches* (New York: Harper & Brothers, 1960) p. 23.
5. Jesse L. Jackson, *Straight from the Heart* (Philadelphia: Fortress Press, 1987), p. xx.
6. Jesse Jackson, Keynote Address to the Democratic National Convention, July 19, 1988.
7. Ibid.
8. Harrell, *Pat Robertson*, p. 210.
9. Ibid., p. 175.
10. Pat Robertson, *America's Date with Destiny* (Nashville: Thomas Nelson, 1986), p. 252.
11. Harrell, *Pat Robertson*, p. 117.
12. Ibid., pp. 202, 205.

13. Jesse Jackson, Announcement of Candidacy for President in 1984 (Speech given at the Washington, D.C. Convention Center).
14. Ibid.
15. Jesse Jackson, Address to the Annual Convention of the Alpha Kappa Alpha Sorority (Speech given at the Washington, D.C. Convention Center, 1985).
16. Jackson, *Straight from the Heart,* pp. 4-5.

7. Prophecies: Political Armageddon or Religious Renaissance?

1. The quotes illustrating the positions of the religious right reflect research done by The People for the American Way, a three hundred thousand member nonprofit constitutional liberties organization based in Washington, D.C. See: *Hostile Climate* (1994); *The Religious Right's Campaign Against Sexuality Education* (1994); *A Turn to the Right* (1994) and occasional papers (1994): "Religious Right's Efforts at Outreach to Ethnic and Minority Communities," "State and Local Antigay Initiatives and Legislative Reports," "The Religious Right in the Republican Party," and "The New Crusade for School Prayer Trampling Religious Liberty."

Conclusion

1. Joint Center for Political Studies, "Conference Report of the Fourth National Policy Institute," Vol. 12, No. 4, (April 1984), p. 7.